The Greater Pittsburgh region looked much different prior to the Industrial Revolution. This sketch by Mrs. James Gibson, of Philadelphia, was published in the *History of Allegheny County, Pennsylvania*, and depicts Pittsburgh as it appeared around 1817. The aforementioned book describes the growth of the country west of the Appalachian Mountains as being "something phenomenal." (Courtesy of the Allegheny Foothills Historical Society.)

ON THE COVER: A family poses for a photographer with evidence of the valley's industrial prominence rising behind them in the form of gas wells. This photograph is believed to have been taken on or in the vicinity of Walnut Street in what is now Versailles Borough. (Courtesy of the McKeesport Regional History and Heritage Center.)

IMAGES
of America

OLD VERSAILLES
TOWNSHIP

Frank J. Kordalski Jr. and
Michael R. Kordalski

ARCADIA
PUBLISHING

Published by Arcadia Publishing
Charleston, South Carolina

Library of Congress Control Number: 2014957240

For all general information, please contact Arcadia Publishing:
Telephone 843-853-2070
Fax 843-853-0044
E-mail sales@arcadiapublishing.com
For customer service and orders:
Toll-Free 1-888-313-2665

Visit us on the Internet at www.arcadiapublishing.com

We would like to dedicate this book to our grandmother, Elaine
Kukurin, who passed away in the midst of our writing of this book.
She provided us with much support, many historic images, and
always kept us well fed. We will always love and remember you.

We would also like to dedicate this book to two furry
members of our family, Bitsy and Pika. We hope to
see you again someday at the rainbow bridge.

CONTENTS

ACKNOWLEDGMENTS

We have many people to whom we are indebted. First, to our family, all of whom have given us much encouragement throughout this project, we thank you. Second, we would like to thank the volunteers, board of directors, and staff of the McKeesport Regional History and Heritage Center, especially Michelle Wardle-Eggers, Gail Waite, and John Barna.

We would also like to especially thank the following individuals: Jim and Linda Wetzler (who initially encouraged the lead author to write a book on the White Oak/Versailles area), George and Louise Beswick, Rev. Eric Dennis, Irene Young, Judy and Ralph Rosensteel, Loran Bohman, Rev. Richard Krug, Debra Maurizi, Connie Rosenbayger, Claire Hildenbrand, Fr. Jack Brennan, and Paula Mullen.

To all of the individuals, groups, and organizations not specifically mentioned who allowed us to utilize your photographs in our book (and pick your brains for information relating to said photographs), know that we thank you most heartily.

Images from the McKeesport Regional History and Heritage Center are noted throughout the book as being courtesy of "MRHHC." Unless otherwise noted, all images in this book appear courtesy of the authors.

INTRODUCTION

The original Township of Versailles was one of the seven original townships created during the first meeting of the Allegheny County court on September 24, 1788. The other townships included the new county seat, Pittsburgh; Plum; St. Clair; Moon; Mifflin; and Elizabeth. At this time, the boundaries of the township were set as follows, according to *History of Allegheny County, Pennsylvania:* "Beginning at the mouth of the Youghiogheny river [sic], thence up said river to the mouth of Brush creek [sic], thence down Turtle creek [sic] to the mouth thereof, thence up the Monongahela river [sic] to the place of the beginning." The township was named after the Palace of Versailles, France, in recognition of the assistance provided by the French during the American Revolution.

Over the years, boundaries changed and new communities formed. Seven communities (the city of McKeesport, North Versailles and South Versailles Townships, and the boroughs of East McKeesport, Versailles, Wall, and White Oak) were entirely carved from the boundaries of the original Versailles Township. Parts of two other communities—Wilmerding and Trafford Boroughs—were also taken from the original boundaries of Versailles Township.

The scope of this book aims to analyze the history of the communities that arose out of this "old" Versailles Township. Of course, space limitations inevitably exist. If a favorite local park, family church, or relative's house is not pictured within *Old Versailles Township*, the authors sincerely apologize. Several other books exist that deal with other surrounding communities, and in the hopes of not overlapping information and images found in Images of America: *McKeesport* and Postcard History Series: *McKeesport*, McKeesport will not have its own chapter. (Fear not, for McKeesport played a major role in the development of the area and will be alluded to via various images and captions). Also, for much the same reason, the communities of the Turtle Creek Valley (Wilmerding, Wall, and Trafford) will not be focused on as much as the others given the existence of Images of America: *Wilmerding and the Westinghouse Air Brake Company.* With that said, the authors digress.

The area that would become Versailles Township was originally contested territory. First, the British and French fought over what is now Allegheny County during the Seven Years' War (also known as the French and Indian War). Later, the colonies of Pennsylvania and Virginia debated who had ultimate control of the region surrounding Fort Pitt; in 1780, the two entities reached an agreement that gave the area to Pennsylvania.

Versailles Township began in 1788—like the other six townships of Allegheny County—as a forested, highly agricultural (but sparsely populated) settlement. As more settlers arrived in the waning years of the 18th century, agricultural endeavors continued to be the backbone of the region. Farmers' passion for their way of life in this area even incurred the displeasure of the federal government, resulting in the Whiskey Rebellion in the 1790s.

After McKeesport became its own borough in 1841, the first division of the old Versailles Township occurred between northern and southern communities in 1869. According to the *History of Allegheny County, Pennsylvania,* the population of Versailles was 5,293 in 1860. Because the centers of population were so spread out, particularly with Port Perry in the northwest and Coulter in the southeast, a division of the township was almost inevitable. In an 1869 petition in favor of the division of the township, the county government settled upon the following boundary during its April sessions: "Beginning on Westmoreland county line near the house of John Ludwig, and running thence by the cross-roads near James Black's to the Monongahela river above Saltsburg."

South Versailles was the first of the two newly created townships that saw the next division—in 1875, the second precinct petitioned to be set up as a separate township; thus, the "new" Versailles Township was born. At this time, the area surrounding the villages of Alpsville, Emblem, and Coulter became the sole remainder of South Versailles Township. The south-central part of the township broke away in 1892 and became Versailles Borough.

The North Versailles area, too, began to fragment into individual municipalities. In 1893, a petition was presented during the December session of Allegheny County court requesting the formation of a new borough. From this petition, East McKeesport was born. The first council met at the home of H.G. Curry on March 2, 1896; the members of the original council were Oscar E. Lindbom, John T. Muse, Harvey S. Welsh, H.J. Harris, H.G. Curry, W.S. Brashear, and G.B. Watkins; James Carson was the first burgess.

Wilmerding and Wall do not comprise an extremely large portion of the original township, but they are situated along Turtle Creek. The Turtle Creek valley saw a dramatic increase in industrialization during the 1890s. In 1887 and 1888, George Westinghouse purchased land in the Turtle Creek valley for use as an improved site for his Westinghouse Air Brake Company. Westinghouse sold the land to the East Pittsburgh Improvement Company for the purpose of developing the site, and the company began to sell plots of land in 1889. Wilmerding officially became a borough on March 8, 1890. What is now the north side of Wilmerding originally was part of Patton Township (now Monroeville).

The borough of Wall received its name from the Walls family (they later changed their name to "Wall"), who owned much of the land that would become the community. In 1829, James Walls purchased the family farm that was later passed to his sons Henry and John Walls. Henry and John lived in a log cabin near the center of present-day Wall. In the early 1840s, Walls' Station opened on the Pennsylvania Railroad. The name was eventually shortened to "Wall Station." Henry and John sold their property to their cousin Frank Wall, an engineer on riverboats. Frank developed the property, and Wall Station incorporated as Wall Borough in 1904.

While doing research for this book, a particular quote caught the authors' eyes. Taken from the *Versailles Borough Centennial* booklet, it nicely sums up our work on this volume: "Many of the photographs show Versailles as it appears today . . . One must remember, however, that the Versailles of today will someday be the Versailles of the past." We have attempted to capture as much of the past as possible in the space allotted to us. There is much more history that we wish we could have included, but we fear there is not enough paper for the creation of such a book. However, we hope that this will only encourage readers to go out and conduct their own research and make their own historical discoveries. In doing so, we know that they will probably have as much fun as we did while writing this book. Enjoy!

One

EARLY HISTORY

Swamps and dense forests would have given the region around old Versailles Township a very different appearance than the one of today. The population in the vicinity of Fort Duquesne was sparse, but the Delaware Indians found the area near the confluence of the Monongahela and Youghiogheny Rivers very favorable for their hunting expeditions. The few European settlers located in the vicinity at the time—mostly French hunters and fur trappers—tended to stay close to Fort Duquesne.

Both the French and the British realized that having control of the waterways surrounding Fort Duquesne had the potential of opening up the entire eastern portion of the continent to trade and colonization. The 1755 expedition led by Gen. Edward Braddock attempted to wrest control of the area away from the French, but Braddock's forces were defeated near the present-day site of the borough of Braddock. The victory claimed during the 1758 expedition led by Gen. John Forbes spelled the beginning of the end of French influence in the area.

Capt. William Shaw is credited as one of the earliest surveyors in the area. Around 1763, Shaw surveyed the area that would become the Bryn Mawr section of White Oak. Upon the creation of Versailles Township by the newly formed Allegheny County government in 1788, frontiersmen slowly began to make their way into the area. By 1790, there were 24 families residing there. An article in the March 9, 1933, *Pittsburgh Press* said of the area: "[It] was rugged but there were some excellent farms and much rich bottom land. Settlers were few and settlements even fewer."

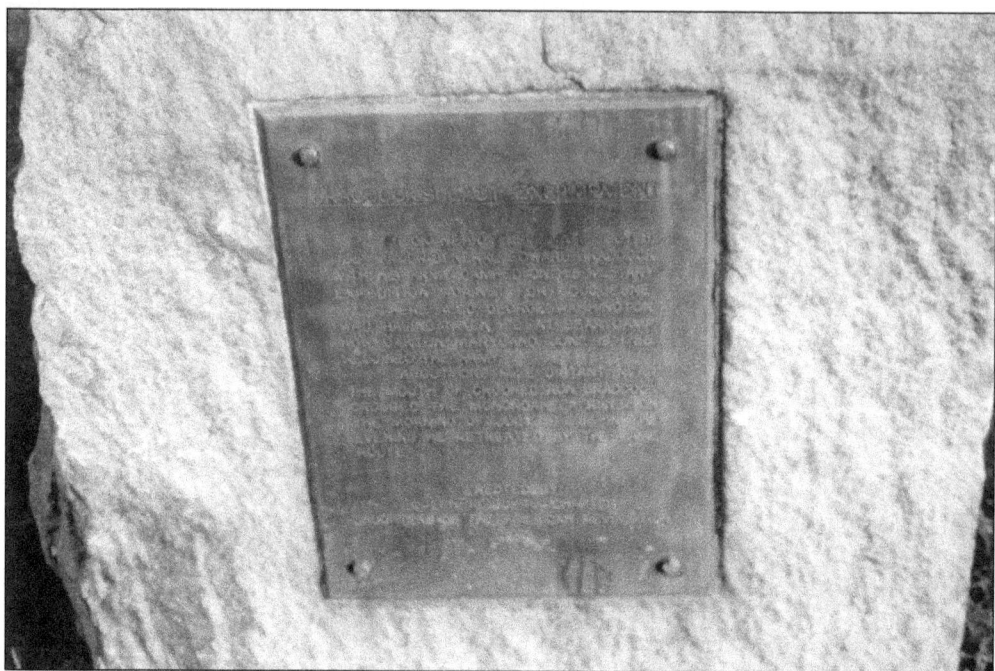

Most students from the McKeesport area are aware of the fact that Gen. Edward Braddock and a young George Washington passed through the area in 1755. This plaque, which is currently situated at White Oak's Heritage Hill Pool, states that approximately "one-mile distant, at the mouth of Crooked Run Creek, Braddock crossed the Monongahela on the morning of July 19, 1755. In the evening, he retreated by the same route." Crooked Run Creek, which forms near the intersection of Foster Road and Route 30 in North Versailles, spills into the Monongahela near the McKeesport-Duquesne Bridge.

At one time, Crooked Run Creek emptied directly into the Monongahela River at this point. Industrialization—in the form of train tracks and roadways (like the McKeesport-Duquesne Bridge)—has long since covered over the site. Construction began on the McKeesport-Duquesne Bridge in 1926, and it was completed in 1928. (MRHHC.)

No. 56 Braddock Road and White Oak Level Road, near McKeesport, Pa.

Braddock Road—built in 1755—was constructed by troops of the Virginia militia and British regulars commanded by Gen. Edward Braddock as part of an expedition to wrest control of the region from the French. The above postcard shows a man sitting at the point at which Braddock's Road comes off the high ground from Stewartsville and intersects with White Oak Level Road (now Lincoln Way). Pictured below is the bridge along Lincoln Way as it crosses Long Run (near Oak Park Mall). This bridge was near the locale where Sampson's Mill had formerly been situated. (John Barna.)

No. 57 Bridge over Long Run, near Samson's Old Mill, near McKeesport, Pa.

11

At the site of this spring (near the intersection of O'Neil Boulevard and Summit Avenue), Gen. Edward Braddock's force made its last encampment on July 8, 1755. George Washington, who had previously taken ill near Little Meadows, rejoined the expedition at this site. The spring was later destroyed by development in the area. (John Barna.)

Pictured here are Queen Aliquippa's Rocks. On July 9, 1755, Gen. Edward Braddock and his forces crossed the Monongahela River at or near the spot where Crooked Run Creek empties into the river. Queen Aliquippa is said to have warned Braddock against proceeding with an attack against the French (although, in actuality, Queen Aliquippa had died in 1754). (John Barna.)

12

Two

NORTH VERSAILLES TOWNSHIP

The growth of Port Perry in the north and Coulterville in the south was a major factor that led to the decision to split the northern and southern parts of the township. In subsequent decades, other areas that became population centers include Saltsburgh and Allequippa Grove, along the Monongahela River; Pleasant Hill (near what is now East McKeesport); Point Pleasant, located near the current intersections of Route 30 and McKee Road; Stewart's Station; Spring Hill; Mosside Station; and Wall Station.

Although North Versailles would later lose territory due to the formation of the boroughs of East McKeesport, Wall, Wilmerding, and Trafford, it has many distinct neighborhoods, including Park Terrace, Arlington, South Wilmerding, Green Valley, West Wilmerding, Dixon Hollow, and Crestas Terrace.

North Versailles was largely an agricultural town well into the 20th century. The Taylors, Nasers, Parks, Hoffmans, Millers and Kukurins are just a few of the families that owned farmland in North Versailles. Gradually, Greensburg Pike—which had served local farmers as a route to all points east or west—evolved from a two-lane road to a four-lane highway. Shopping centers, churches, and businesses began replacing the fields and farmhouses.

Although North Versailles is not quite as large in square mileage as it was in 1869, it is now currently about 8.3 square miles and, as of the 2010 census, has a population of over 10,200. Several notable residents have come from the North Versailles area. Most Pittsburgh-area chocolate aficionados will recognize the name David L. Clark, founder of the D.L. Clark Company. Clark once lived in what is now the Fairhaven neighborhood. The Clark family's old mansion still exists, as well as the house that served as their gatehouse (along Foster Road). Comedienne Donna Jean Young—who briefly appeared on Rowan and Martin's *Laugh-In*—grew up in the Arlington section of town. Jazz drummer Jeff "Tain" Watts and former Tampa Bay Buccaneers/Los Angeles Rams wide receiver Gordon Jones were also from North Versailles.

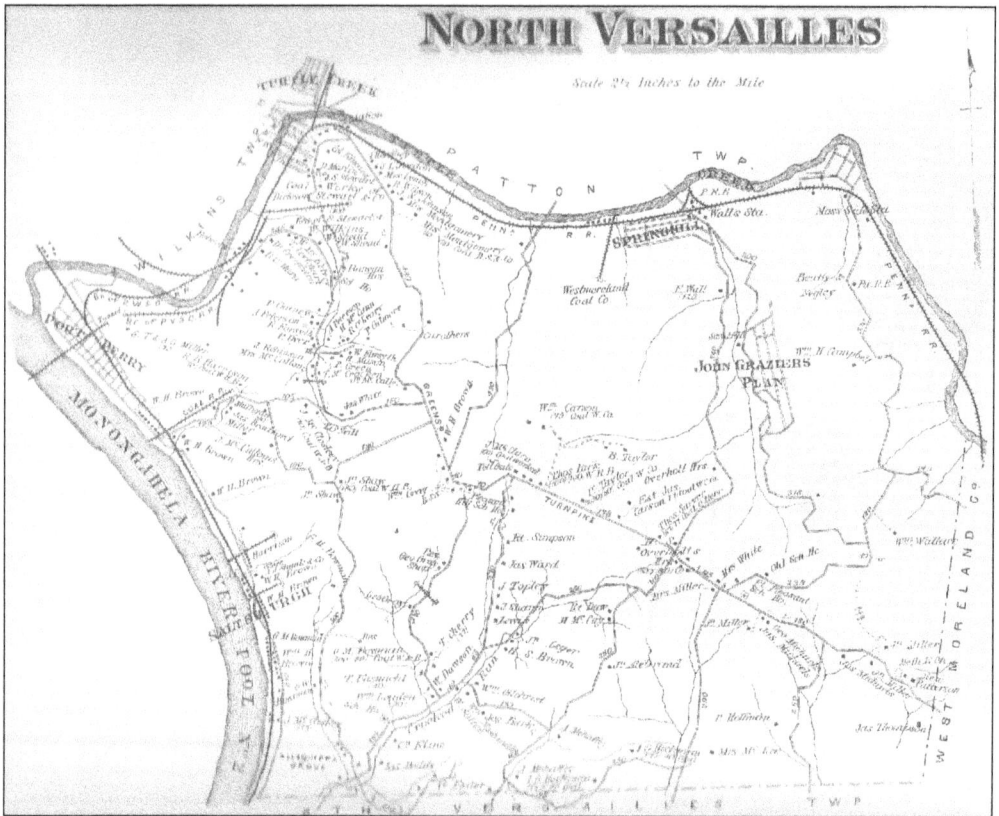

This map of the North Versailles Township area was included in the 1988 reprint of the 1876 *Atlas of the County of Allegheny, Penna.* (Thomas and Katherine Detre Library and Archives—Senator John Heinz History Center and the Allegheny Foothills Historical Society.)

Pictured here is the grave of Civil War veteran (and North Versailles native) Pvt. Jacob J. Soles. Soles was one of the six soldiers who carried the mortally wounded Pres. Abraham Lincoln from Ford's Theatre. Later in life, he would often sit—in his Civil War uniform—on the porch of his house along Greensburg Pike recounting the story of that fateful night.

This undated photograph shows a westbound view of what is now US Route 30. The photograph was taken near the old Hoffman Road, near where the Winchester Room later stood. The hill in the upper right corner of the photograph would have been the vicinity where the Naser family's farm stood. (John Barna.)

Several coke ovens (now on private property) can still be seen along Fifth Avenue in North Versailles. It is not known which operation owned these ovens, however, the Bowman [Coal] Mine once existed near the North Versailles–McKeesport border. An 1899 *Daily News* article touted that the Bowman Mine had "enough coal in the tract to supply the majority of McKeesport's retail trade for 20 or 25 years." (John Barna.)

The Naser family owned a farm near the present-day site of the North Versailles Giant Eagle (hence, the nearby road is named Naser Road). During the early 19th century, in the era of stagecoach lines, there was once a foot path from the present-day location of Valley Avenue in Wall through the hollow and across Naser's farm to the stagecoach stop tollgate. The stagecoach line eventually ran from Philadelphia to Pittsburgh.

The intersection—shown here in a view from St. John the Baptist Parish Cemetery—of Crooked Run Road (lower right), Foster Road (behind the tree line), and Broad Street (top center) is located near the spring from which Crooked Run Creek forms. Heading south on Foster Road would lead a traveler to the Fairhaven neighborhood. Before it was a developed neighborhood, the Fairhaven area was home to David Lytle Clark, founder of the D.L. Clark Company.

Tony Kukurin and Pauline Duchik Kukurin, pictured above on the day of their wedding (sometime prior to 1911) had quite a journey to the New World. Tony came from Austrian-controlled Croatia to America to earn money; after boarding with his sister and brother-in-law, Helen and Lewis Drnjevich, in Connellsville, he eventually sent for Pauline to join him. Tony later worked in a butcher's shop in Export before making his way to North Versailles and buying an 18-acre tract of farmland from Isaac Taylor. On this land, Tony operated a farm for the next two decades before semiretiring.

Both Tony and Pauline lived good, long lives—Tony passed away in 1977 at age 93, and Pauline lived to be 106. The photograph of Pauline at right was taken sometime around her 100th birthday.

Tony Kukurin poses with a mule on his farm. A comical story recounted by Tony's son, Rudy, involves an instance when Tony was trying to lead the mule either to or from the barn, but said mule refused to go along with his master. The beast of burden instead planted his hoof on Tony's foot, and no amount of coaxing could prompt the mule to move. (Elaine Kukurin.)

Sometime in the 1960s, Elaine Dency Kukurin and her brother-in-law Joe Zavalydriga posed for this photograph in her driveway. The building on the hill behind them sits along US Route 30 and served many purposes over the years, including housing McBride's Garage. The building currently houses a day care and some apartments. (Elaine Kukurin.)

In 1942, Rudy and Elaine Kukurin (center) pose with their wedding party in the yard of Rudy's parents, Tony and Pauline, along what is now US Route 30. Before it was known as US Route 30, it was the Lincoln Highway, and instead of being four-plus lanes along much of its length, it was a two-lane road. (Elaine Kukurin.)

Members of the Kukurin family take a well-deserved break from celebrating at a family gathering. Pictured here from left to right are Vince Eiseman, Emma Kukurin Eiseman, Pauline Kukurin, Rudy Kukurin, and Elaine Kukurin.

The building in the foreground once served as an office for Frank Kukurin and Sons Contracting. The structure in the background—now home to an insurance agency—was the home of Pauline and Tony Kukurin. After subdividing the farm in the 1940s along what is now lower Third Street in North Versailles, Tony gave each of his four children a quarter-acre lot to do with as they pleased.

Appreciation for the outdoors was often something passed down from generation to generation. The authors of this book are no exception. In this c. 1985 photograph, Rudy Kukurin Sr. and grandson Frank Kordalski Jr. celebrate the day's catch at Twin Lakes Park in nearby Greensburg. In the latter part of the 20th century, as Allegheny County became more populous, people came to more rural counties in order to find the proverbial "peace and quiet."

Rudy Kukurin Sr. poses with his children Rudy Jr. and Karen. The structures in the background once served as a shed and chicken coop for the old family farm. Although this particular family ceased their involvement in farming in the 1950s, other local families continued to rely on income drawn from agricultural pursuits. The authors' parents have memories of visiting a small farm along Upper Heckman Road (along North Versailles/White Oak border) from whom they would purchase eggs. Although no longer operational, parts of the chicken coop still stand today. (Elaine Kukurin.)

St. Nicholas Byzantine Catholic Church, located in downtown McKeesport, has a cemetery several miles away from its church building. The cemetery, located on the cusp of what was once farmland, was founded sometime in the early 1900s. Given the close proximity of the graveyard to his family's farm, Rudy Kukurin Sr. recounted to the authors that he would occasionally see members of the congregation picnicking in the clearing above the cemetery after tending to their family members' graves. The clearing has become much more occupied over the decades and is also now the site of a small chapel used during funerals. Also pictured below are several children and the parish priest from St. Nicholas. (Below, MRHHC.)

Founded around the turn of the 20th century, the original St. Nicholas Byzantine Catholic Church congregation primarily consisted of Rusyns but also contained people of Ukrainian, Hungarian, and Romanian descent. Many of these ethnicities branched off to form their own churches. Seen here in the 1940s, several men from the congregation pose for a photograph with the parish priest. (MRHHC.)

St. John the Baptist Ukrainian Catholic Church of McKeesport also has its parish cemetery in North Versailles. The cemetery is adjacent to the St. Nicholas Byzantine Catholic Church's cemetery. Seen here are a memorial stone and benches located near the front gate of the cemetery along Crooked Run Road.

Although this particular well—located along Crooked Run Road near the St. John the Baptist Ukrainian Catholic Church's cemetery—is more decorative than functional, wells were a central part of any farm. A spring helped supply the nearby Kukurin farm with water in the 1920s and 1930s.

Railroads played an integral part in the history of this region, especially with the major roles that coal, steel, and manufacturing had in the area. This train car, however, has not traveled the rails for quite some time; it has spent the last few decades parked behind Design Monuments, and it housed a travel agent's office for many years.

Pauline Kukurin's health began to wane after her 100th birthday, but her mind remained sharp throughout her 106 years. Not long after the death of her husband, Tony, in 1977, she went to North Carolina to live with her eldest daughter, Lydia Schoderbek. Pauline died December 1, 1992.

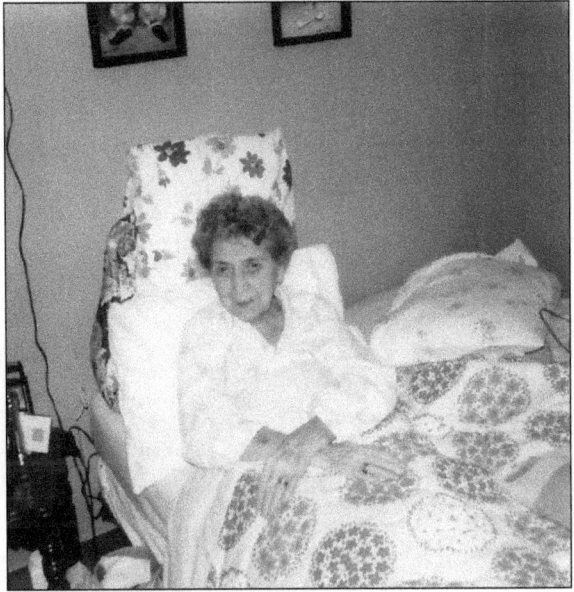

The Grandview Cemetery sign is easily visible from US Route 30 in North Versailles. On the opposite corner of the intersection is the former Matt's Furniture building, and behind that is the Sunset Volunteer Fire Department. In 1999, Sunset merged with the Dixon Hollow and Green Valley Fire Departments to form the Fire Department of North Versailles. North Versailles is also served by two other fire departments—one in Crestas Terrace and one in the West Wilmerding neighborhood.

North Versailles Crestas Terrace neighborhood was developed in the 1920s as a community for African Americans who worked in the local steel mills. The Crestas Terrace Volunteer Fire Department was founded on August 27, 1927, as one of the first entirely African American volunteer fire companies in Pennsylvania. The company began with 14 volunteers. The first line officers were Matthew Jones (chief), Santee Powell Sr. (captain), William Pearson (first lieutenant), and Albert Hopkin (second lieutenant). The department trustees were James E. Askew Sr., John W. Askew, Jesse (Fritz) Carter, and Champ Brooks. In the early years of Crestas Terrace, conditions were very trying; the area had shoddy roads and no city water, so fires were fought via "bucket brigade." The company received its first hand-drawn chemical tank from Westinghouse Electric Company, and, in 1937, purchased its first motor-driven equipment, a 1918 Cadillac (nicknamed "Old Betsy"). (Paula Mullen.)

The Crestas Terrace Volunteer Fire Department broke ground for a new building in April 1937, and its construction was complete in 1938. The members of the Crestas Terrace Volunteer Fire Department are pictured here in the 1950s (above) and the 1960s (below). In 1942, the department purchased a 1938 Chevy chassis, and under the supervision of Joseph Jackson, the chassis was used to build a streamlined truck fully equipped for fighting all types of fires. The area that makes up Crestas Terrace, which is situated above the site where the Port Perry neighborhood once existed, was originally farmland owned by the Miller family. (Paula Mullen.)

Blue Dell, a popular entertainment venue, was located just over the Westmoreland County line in North Huntington Township. The complex had a swimming pool, a diner, and a drive-in theater. The theater had a 500-car capacity. Blue Dell opened in 1949 and closed in 1984. (MRHHC.)

Pictured here is the family (and homestead) of W.C. Cronemeyer in Highland Grove. Those pictured are (from left to right): Henry, Molly C. (seated), W.C. (holding William), Ernest (on fence), Caroline C., Malvina Havecotte Cronmeyer (W.C.'s second wife), and Johanna. Molly, Caroline, and Johanna were later known by their married names of McElroy, Spalding, and Hunter, respectively. (MRHHC.)

The Highland Grove neighborhood was part of North Versailles prior to being annexed by the City of McKeesport. According to legend, it was in this area that George Washington met with the Seneca Queen Aliquippa. According to the December 31, 1753, journal entry of Washington, "As we intended to take horses here, and it required some time to find them, I went up about three miles to the mouth of the Youghiogheny to visit Queen Alliquippa [sic], who had expressed great concern that we passed her in going to the fort. I made her a present of a match-coat and a bottle of rum, [of] which [the] latter was thought much the best present of the two."

GREEN VALLEY
PRIMARY SCHOOL

WE ARE GRE EN VAL LEY

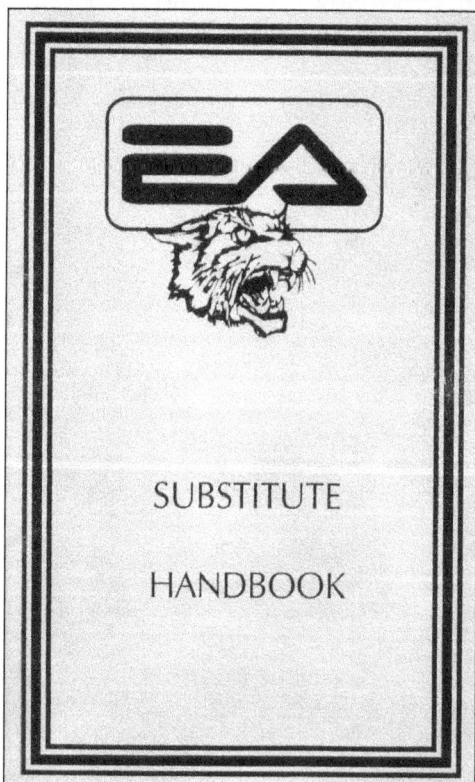

SUBSTITUTE

HANDBOOK

Immediately prior to publication of this book, Green Valley Elementary School had been the oldest school in use in the East Allegheny School District. As of 2015, the school was closed. The first school in the township was Point Pleasant (a one-room schoolhouse that housed eight grades). Other early schools included Port Perry, Saltsburg, Bowman, Spring Hill Nos. 1 and 2, Oak Hill, and North McKeesport.

Pictured here is a recent handbook for substitute teachers working in the East Allegheny School District (EASD). EASD serves the communities of East McKeesport, North Versailles, Wall, and Wilmerding. After the formation of the district (known as Westinghouse Valley Area Schools from 1962 to 1966), Westinghouse Memorial High School served as the district's official high school until East Allegheny High School was built in 1969.

This area is rich in its ethnic and religious diversity. Pictured here are scenes from the Holy Family Polish National Catholic Church cemetery located off of Naysmith Road in North Versailles. The parish (located in McKeesport) was founded on September 16, 1921. The parish celebrated its first Mass on Christmas in 1921 at the remodeled church building at the corner of Market and Buena Vista Streets in McKeesport. (The congregation moved into its current building, located along Eden Park Boulevard, on May 4, 1967). On March 4, 1923, the parish cemetery was established with the purchase of seven acres of land at the corner of Foster and Naysmith Roads. Bishop Leon Grochowski blessed the land in 1924.

St. Mary's Cemetery (located along the border between White Oak and North Versailles) is the cemetery of McKeesport's St. Mary Czestochowa parish. Founded by Polish immigrants in 1893, St. Mary's went on to erect a school in 1935 and a new church building in 1954. In 2010, the parish merged with the St. Martin de Porres and St. Pius V Parishes to form Corpus Christi Parish.

Pictured here is the Gemilas Chesed Cemetery (located next to St. Mary's Cemetery). The cement container shown here contains visitation stones. Placing stones on Jewish graves is an ancient custom performed as an act of remembrance. Many people place flowers on graves—flowers that, like life itself, wither. Stones, like eternal memories, do not.

Grandview Cemetery was founded in 1900 on land purchased from the Overholt and Fechtner families. The 194-acre community cemetery, located along Greensburg Pike (now US Route 30), was chartered as the Grandview Cemetery Association (a nonprofit organization) on July 12, 1902. The first board of managers included Harry D. Patch (president), Dr. George L. Beswick (secretary), and Jesse H. Cunningham (treasurer), among others. Grandview is also known for having regular Memorial Day services. During services held on May 30, 1935, Grandview Cemetery presented a large plot of land at the entrance of the cemetery for use by military veterans; the area is known as the Flag Pole Triangle.

View in Grand View Cemetery, East McKeesport, Pa.

Grandview Cemetery is the final resting place of many local residents. By 1940, Grandview and New St. Joseph's Cemeteries had hosted approximately 11,000 burials. Pictured at left is a monument belonging to the Taylor family. The Taylors owned vast swaths of land in the area, including the area west of the cemetery (part of which became the Taylor housing plan). The building behind the skinny, obelisk-like monument is the Grandview Cemetery chapel. Although Grandview is largely a non-sectarian cemetery, in April 1936, the St. Nicholas Serbian Orthodox Church of Wilmerding requested that a portion of the cemetery (pictured below) be set aside for their use. The church's pastor, Rev. Milovan P. Shundich, led the effort to lay out this section.

The New St. Joseph's Cemetery was founded in 1912, when St. Peter's Catholic Church (in McKeesport) wanted to expand their existing cemetery; "Old" St. Joseph Cemetery was located on Coursin Street. The church purchased 40 acres of Grandview Cemetery, and John Lovett was named the sexton of the cemetery. This monument stands between the three newest mausoleums, which were built in 1994, 1996, and 2012.

This is the original mausoleum, which was built for the New St. Joseph's Cemetery in 1980. Behind the mausoleum is the cemetery office, which was once the sexton's residence. By 2008, the New St. Joseph's Cemetery contained over 25,000 internments.

Shown from afar is Praise Assembly Church of God. Originally founded in McKeesport in 1943, the congregation moved into the old Sunset School building during the pastorate of Rev. Al Rowan in the late 1970s. The businesses shown in the lower part of the photograph are located along Crooked Run Road.

All Souls Episcopal Church was formed around 1961 from merger of St. Mary's (of Braddock), St. Alban's (of Duquesne), and St. Margaret's (of Wilmerding). The new congregation worshipped in Sunset Fire Hall for two years before breaking ground on their new building on October 6, 1963. Pictured here is the architect's rendering of the new building. (All Souls Episcopal Church.)

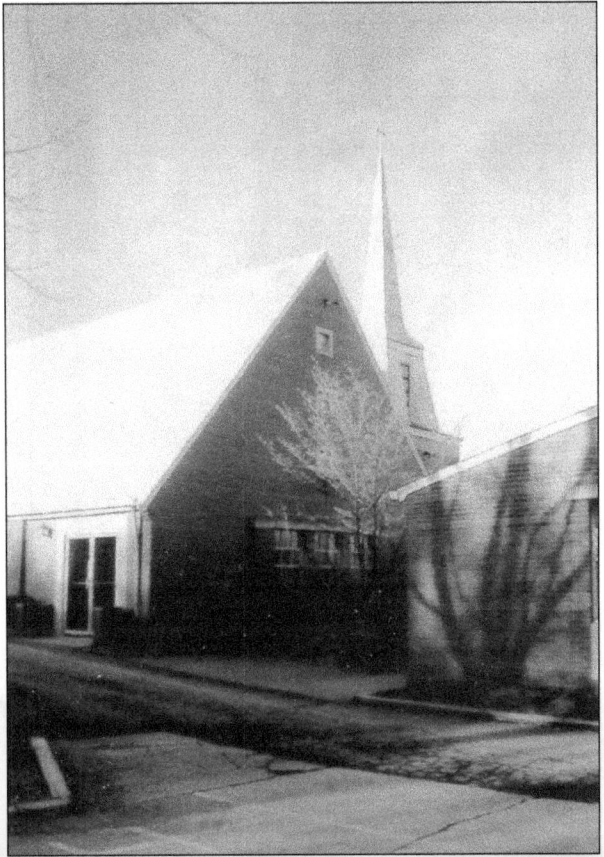

The completed All Souls Episcopal Church is pictured at right. After worshipping in Sunset Fire Hall, the congregation briefly moved worship services to the Masonic Hall in North Versailles's Arlington section prior to the completion of the new building. The first services were held in the new building at the end of October 1964. Below is a view of the sanctuary decorated for Christmas in 1971. (All Souls Episcopal Church.)

Rev. Peter Moore, the first rector for the new congregation of All Souls Episcopal Church, is pictured here with an unidentified parishioner. Reverend Moore celebrated the first service in the rectory on August 13, 1961. Rev. A.W. Evans replaced Reverend Moore in 1963 and oversaw the completion of the new church building and the next 17 years of the church's history. (All Souls Episcopal Church.)

The First Presbyterian Church of East McKeesport, founded in 1897 by members of Long Run Presbyterian Church (now Calvin Presbyterian Church) in North Huntingdon, was originally located at the corner of Fifth Avenue and Lincoln Highway in East McKeesport. The structure pictured here was built in 1900 and razed in 1937 to make way for a gas station. The organ for the church was donated by Andrew Carnegie. (Linway United Presbyterian Church.)

After outgrowing their original church building, the First Presbyterian Church of East McKeesport secured a new parcel of land a few blocks east on Lincoln Highway in June 1930. The date stone for the education wing was dedicated on January 15, 1939. Upon its completion in 1955, the sanctuary came to house 14 beautiful stained-glass windows. The window shown here stands above the chancel; its theme is "Come Unto Me." The photograph of the church exterior was taken for use as the cover of the 1997 church directory. In early 1959, the First Presbyterian Church of East McKeesport changed its name to Linway United Presbyterian Church because of the merger between the Presbyterian Church in the United States of America and the United Presbyterian Church of North America. "Linway" was derived from an abbreviation of the name of the road on which the church sits: Lincoln Highway.

Linway
United
Presbyterian
Church

North Versailles, Pennsylvania

These photographs were taken during the construction of the First Presbyterian Church of East McKeesport's current sanctuary. The first phase of the new building was the education wing, completed in 1939 on land purchased from the Park Estate along the Lincoln Highway in North Versailles. Construction of the sanctuary began after a meeting of the congregation—held on June 29, 1949—authorized the building committee to proceed with construction plans as funds became available. In the photograph above, steel beams used in the sanctuary's construction can be seen. The photograph below shows that the Giant Eagle market (now located about two miles east of this location) was originally across the street from the church. (Linway United Presbyterian Church.)

The choir of the First Presbyterian Church of East McKeesport is pictured above in the completed chancel sometime in the late 1950s. At this time, the church was still utilizing a rebuilt version of the original pipe organ donated by Andrew Carnegie. After the closing of St. Mary's (German) Roman Catholic Church in McKeesport in the 1990s, First Presbyterian had the opportunity to purchase several pipes from the St. Mary's Tellers Kent organ. (Linway United Presbyterian Church.)

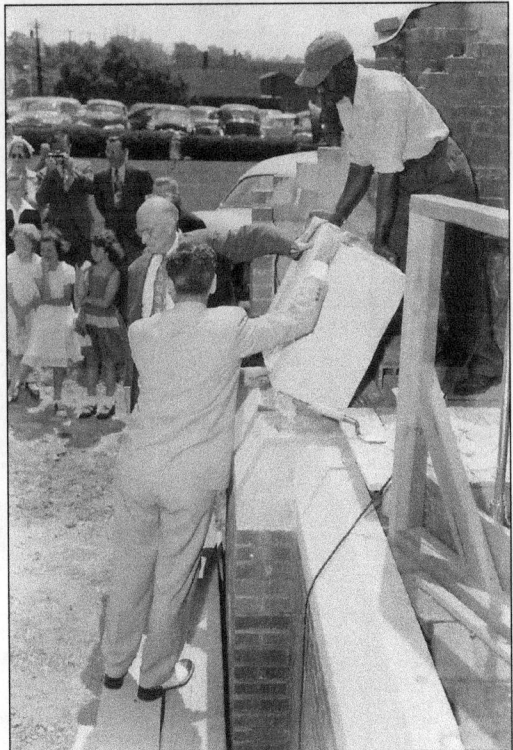

The date stone was dedicated in the midst of the construction of the new sanctuary for the First Presbyterian Church of East McKeesport. At the time this photograph was taken, it would still be several years before the First Presbyterian Church of McKeesport changed its name to Linway United Presbyterian Church. (Linway United Presbyterian Church.)

41

The new sanctuary of the First Presbyterian Church of East McKeesport is progressing nicely in this photograph. The empty window slots would eventually contain 14 stained-glass windows furnished by the Pittsburgh Stained Glass Studios. Six windows depicting various Biblical scenes were installed on each side of the sanctuary, along with one behind the chancel (featuring some of the teachings of Jesus) and one at the back of the narthex (titled "The Resurrection"). (Linway United Presbyterian Church.)

Virginia Beswick was an integral part of Linway United Presbyterian Church for many decades, including as a founding member of the East McKeesport branch of Meals on Wheels. Here, she inspects a quilt at a ladies' function in 1988. (Linway United Presbyterian Church.)

Many St. John's Evangelical Lutheran Church parishioners gathered for this outdoor service (perhaps the laying of the date stone on September 9, 1951?) during the building of the new church. Note the First Presbyterian Church of East McKeesport sanctuary under construction in the background. Across the street were the Amoco station (once McBride's Garage), Nelson's Memorials (which still exists), and the roof of the building (blocked by the "Auto Parts" sign) that was the residence of Tony and Pauline Kukurin. (St. John's Evangelical Lutheran Church.)

This is an architect's rendering of the new St. John's Evangelical Lutheran Church building along Lincoln Highway. The finalized building was completed in early 1952, and a dedication service was held on the afternoon of February 3, 1952. (St. John's Evangelical Lutheran Church.)

Three

EAST MCKEESPORT
BOROUGH

East McKeesport Borough—like the city of McKeesport—draws its name from the McKee family, founders of the city. David McKee (born in 1710) immigrated to America from Scotland in 1750 with several of his relatives. David's son John (born in 1746) moved to the present-day site of McKeesport and became a land trader.

East McKeesport is situated north-by-northeast of the city of McKeesport. As described in the East McKeesport Centennial Book, it is located at an altitude of 1,200 feet "on a beautiful plateau sandwiched between the Turtle Creek, Monongahela, and Youghiogheny Valleys."

With large parcels of land being developed by the Monongahela Investment Company, as well as by a man noted in historical accounts as Mr. Stiling, East McKeesport submitted a petition to be set up as an independent borough in December 1893. The petition was signed by the following residents: W.D. Repper, John F. Hughes, James Carson, Elizabeth Carson, George L. Good, Alice A. Good, Harvey S. Welsh, E.W. Gordon, and Lena Gordon.

Despite mainly being a residential community, East McKeesport also had its share of entertainment and recreation. The Urban Theater opened in 1940 with ticket prices originally set at 35¢ for adults and 10¢ for children. The theater building was eventually sold to St. Robert's Church and later inhabited by Irene's Restaurant. The Victory Hotel served the area as a "tourist home"—a place where travelers could spend a night. After the closing of the Victory, a bed and breakfast opened at the corner of Chicora Street and Broadway Avenue.

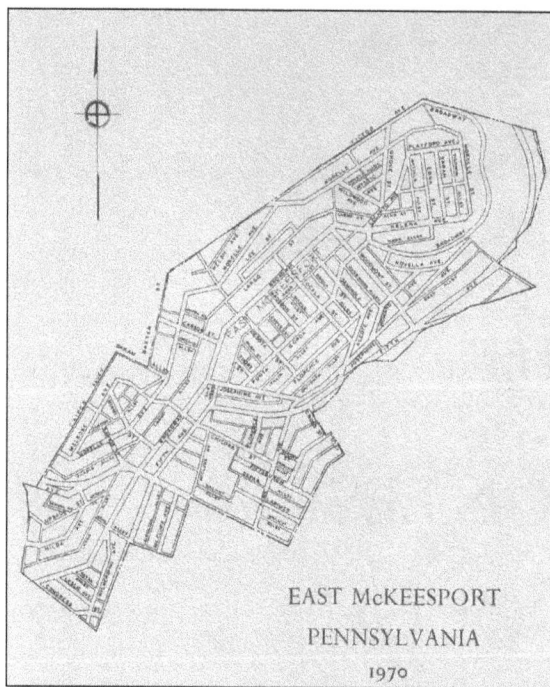

The majority of the four-tenths of a square mile that contain East McKeesport was originally part of the farms of James McClure and James Carson, who transferred ownership to the Monongahela Investment Company on July 5, 1892. This is the map printed in East McKeesport's 75th-anniversary booklet. (Borough of East McKeesport.)

This undated image looks north along Broadway Avenue in East McKeesport. This must be an early photograph, because not long after the borough was incorporated in 1895, the borough council granted the Pittsburgh Railway Company the right to lay tracks on Broadway Avenue. The fare was set at 5¢, and service was available every 10 minutes. The tracks were later moved from Broadway Avenue to Fifth Avenue. (MRHHC.)

46

Congratulations on your . . .

50th ANNIVERSARY

FOODS **CLOVER · FARM STORES** MEATS

Come in - Neighbor

CLOVER FARM STORES

Drop in and see us, Good Neighbor, and notice how well our stores are stocked; how quickly you can obtain everything you need in foods and household needs. Notice too that everything is spic and span; that merchandise is fresh and of finest quality

Wm. HARBOURT & DAN WILLIAMS CLOVER FARM STORES

Clover Farm Stores was located at 1156 Fifth Avenue in East McKeesport. East McKeesport's Fifth Avenue was considered to be the community's business district. This advertisement was published in East McKeesport's 50th-anniversary booklet. (Borough of East McKeesport.)

This bend in US Route 30 is the sign that one is entering East McKeesport. The Victory Hotel (center left) no longer exists; this is now the site of an office/apartment complex. The building in which the Maples resided (behind the trees at center) still exists, although it is now a VFW post. The garage at right also still exists. (MRHHC.)

47

In addition to the Lincoln Highway corridor, Fifth Avenue was the major business district of East McKeesport. Pictured above is Hodgson's Flower Shop, once located at 1014 Fifth Avenue. Leffler's Meat Market, located on US Route 30, was one of the area's earliest stores. Other stores familiar to townspeople over the years are McCall and Hallser, the B&B Market, Star Meat Market, and Lea's Florist. For many years, East McKeesport had two drugstores: Wilson's Drug Store (later known as the East McKeesport Pharmacy), located on Fifth Avenue a few doors from where the Integra Bank once stood, and Jones' Pharmacy, located on Fifth Avenue near Argo Avenue. Pictured at left around 1960, a local bar is in the midst of being demolished. Local landmark the Victory Hotel (pictured on the previous page) was demolished in the 1960s as well. (MRHHC.)

Pictured here is the northern part of the intersection of US Route 30 and Fifth Avenue. This intersection is where the First Presbyterian Church of East McKeesport constructed its first building (before moving a few hundred yards east into North Versailles). Note that the price of gas was only 25¢. (MRHHC.)

Looking southeast, this photograph shows the four service stations that existed at the intersections of Fifth Avenue, Broadway Avenue, and Lincoln Highway in the 1940s. The Get-Go station now stands where the building hiding behind the Esso sign once was; Rite Aid Pharmacy currently stands where the Sunoco station was. (MRHHC.)

Congratulations and Best Wishes to East McKeesport

on her Seventy-Fifth Anniversary from

TOM BESWICK'S ATLANTIC SERVICE

Fifth Avenue and Lincoln Highway

EAST McKEESPORT, PA. 15035

• STATE INSPECTION • DAYTON TIRE CENTER • BATTERIES • ACCESSORIES • LUBRICATION

Phone 823-9998

Local businesses supported the Borough of East McKeesport during its 75th anniversary in 1970. This is the advertisement Tom Beswick's Atlantic Service Station placed in the borough's 75th-anniversary booklet. The station—located at the corner of Fifth Avenue and the Lincoln Highway—was later turned into a Texaco station. (Borough of East McKeesport.)

The East McKeesport Borough Building, located at the intersection of Florence and Josephine Streets, is the home of the borough's government and the police department. Thomas Manning was the borough's first police officer. As an employee of the McKeesport-Wilmerding Railway Company, he was initially tasked with patrolling the railway line between Carson's Grove and the Victory Hotel. William Schaffer was the first police chief. (MRHHC.)

East McKeesport was once served by two fire departments (pictured here): Vigilant Fire Company No. 1 and East McKeesport Volunteer Fire Company No. 2. East McKeesport Volunteer Fire Company No. 2 was organized on March 21, 1921, and granted an official charter from the state in 1930. A frame building constructed at the corner of Broadway and Punta Gorda Avenues housed the new company's equipment and provided a voting place for citizens of the area. The department's first pieces of equipment were a hand-drawn hose cart and a 35-gallon chemical tank. As the borough expanded, the department purchased more modern equipment. In 1943, the borough purchased its first ambulance; it was used during World War II to transport wounded soldiers from the county airport to area hospitals. In 1998, the Wall Volunteer Fire Department and East McKeesport's fire department merged to form the United Volunteer Fire & Rescue. (MRHHC.)

Here, an unidentified member of a veterans' association hands out flags to children. During World War I, almost 90 men from East McKeesport served in the military; during World War II, that number jumped to about 560. The area as a whole has many veterans' associations, including the VFW Post No. 430 (of East McKeesport) and the Gen. Smedley D. Butler American Legion Post 701 (of White Oak). (MRHHC.)

Public School, East McKeesport, Pa.

Prior to the consolidation of smaller school districts in the 1960s, East McKeesport had its own school district. Before the creation of East Allegheny School District, East McKeesport High School was one of the secondary schools North Versailles students had the option of attending. It later became one of East Allegheny's junior high schools, and the school closed in 1982. (MRHHC.)

St. Robert Bellarmine Catholic Church was established in 1950 as a mission of St. Aloysius Parish in Wilmerding. The congregation celebrated its first Mass in East McKeesport on April 12, 1950, in the Urban Theatre on Fifth Avenue. A priest from St. Aloysius came to the Urban Theatre every Sunday to celebrate Mass, and in July 1951 the pastor of St. Aloysius made the decision to purchase the theater and convert it to a church. On September 27, 1951, St. Robert Bellarmine was canonically established as an independent parish. Pictured above in a 1964 photograph is the first-grade class of St. Robert Bellarmine's School. St. Robert Bellarmine's School served students in kindergarten through eighth grade. Pictured below, Fr. Francis Bailey leads a dedication service during ground-breaking activities. (St. Robert Bellarmine Catholic Church.)

In this c. 1959 photograph, Fr. Francis Bailey, along with two unidentified men, poses with two nuns from St. Robert's Parish. The title of the photograph, as presented in St. Robert Bellarmine Catholic Church's 50th-anniversary calendar (printed in 2001) was "St. Robert's Sisters' Green Stamp Car." (St. Robert Bellarmine Catholic Church.)

Pictured here are several of the lunch ladies who served warm meals to countless students during the 30-plus years that St. Robert Bellarmine's School was open. Unfortunately, due to dwindling enrollment, the school closed around 2004. In addition to catechism classes and other church functions, the old school building also serves as a venue for other community functions. (St. Robert Bellarmine Catholic Church.)

Pictured in this undated photograph are members of the altar committee of St. Robert Bellarmine Catholic Church. From left to right are Mary Smialek, Rosemarie Macko, and Valerie Uhrin. Generally, altar committees (or altar guilds) provide care for the sanctuary as a setting for worship. They often pay special attention to items within the chancel area, including flowers, altar brass, and paraments. (St. Robert Bellarmine Catholic Church.)

In this undated photograph, members of the St. Robert Bellarmine Catholic Church parish council's executive board pose for the camera. Pictured from left to right are Grace Miller, Christopher Hoke, Michael Tomko, Fr. John Scanlon, Edward Brannan, Francis Donohue, and Ann Newman. (St. Robert Bellarmine Catholic Church.)

55

Parishioners of St. John's Lutheran Church pose during the parish's Sunday school picnic held in 1908 at the Brown family's farm. The authors were able to use old maps to locate a farm belonging to W.H. Brown and sons, located near the present-day site where Greensburg Pike Section 2 veers off of US Route 30. (St. John's Evangelical Lutheran Church.)

The Sunday school class of 1938 is pictured outside of St. John's Chicora Street building. Pictured from left to right are (first row) Paul Miller, Eleanor Buettner, Byron Eisaman, Richard Gwan, Jean Gilmore, Margie Gilmore, and Audrey Hilt; (second row) Graham Douglas, Marilyn Buettner, Shirley Larson, Laura Longdon, June Douglas, Dorothy Cowan, Dorothy Buettner, Alberta Hilt, and Marlene Blend. Not pictured are teachers Ethel Boone, Ann Anderson, and Louise Frommell. (St. John's Evangelical Lutheran Church.)

St. John's Lutheran Church began in 1903 in East McKeesport. Due to crowded conditions, Sunday school classes had to meet concurrently in the sanctuary, as shown in this undated photograph. This building served the congregation until they moved to their current location—along the Lincoln Highway—in 1952. The Chicora Street building went on to serve the East McKeesport Church of the Brethren. (St. John's Evangelical Lutheran Church.)

This is the residence of F.L. Bolton of East McKeesport. This photograph appears to have been taken sometime in the early 20th century, and it was during this time that many improvements were made to streets in the borough. In 1912, Broadway Avenue was paved; it was topped off with bricks in 1914. In 1927, Punta Gorda Avenue was paved, and Lincoln Highway was improved in 1928. (MRHHC.)

Four

TURTLE CREEK VALLEY

As mentioned in this book's introduction, the original boundaries of Versailles Township—and, later, North Versailles Township—extended to the waterway now known as Turtle Creek. This encompassed the southern area of Wilmerding Borough, all of Wall Borough, and a very tiny portion of Trafford Borough.

To say that George Westinghouse and his business acumen played a minor role in the region's economy would be a major understatement. Westinghouse's Airbrake and Engineering Companies helped make the Turtle Creek valley and its surrounding area an ethnic melting pot.

Westinghouse's original plant—completed in 1870—was situated along Liberty Avenue (between Twenty-fourth and Twenty-fifth Streets) in Pittsburgh. Within a decade, space constraints caused Westinghouse to move his airbrake business to facilities in old Allegheny City (now the North Side of Pittsburgh).

Within 10 years of that move, with ever-increasing demand and production capabilities, Westinghouse purchased approximately 500 acres of farmland in the Turtle Creek Valley. After this purchase, he was able to begin construction on a new factory as well as the borough of Wilmerding itself.

Because of its proximity to both Wilmerding and Pitcairn, Wall Borough citizens found work in both Westinghouse's factory and the railyard across the creek in Pitcairn. The town saw tremendous growth during the first half of the 20th century because of its location near industrial centers. As industry increased in the 1920s, transportation improved, with modern roads connecting Wall, Trafford, and US Route 30. In 1930, the Mosside Bridge was completed, and a two-lane paved boulevard was installed. Because of the road's improvement to two lanes, not only did this improve things for vehicular transit, but it also made it more navigable for bus transit.

GEORGE WESTINGHOUSE
FOUNDER OF WILMERDING

George Westinghouse played a tremendous role in the world of engineering. On September 28, 1869, Westinghouse founded the Westinghouse Airbrake Company after having invented the railway airbrake earlier that year. After first locating his business in the city of Pittsburgh, Westinghouse moved it to the banks of the Turtle Creek (in what is now Wilmerding) in 1889. (*Golden Echoes: 50th Anniversary—Wilmerding, Pennsylvania.*)

The George Westinghouse Memorial Bridge, shown on this 1940s postcard, gave drivers on the Lincoln Highway a much less winding trip across the Turtle Creek Valley. Lincoln Highway officially veered off of present-day US Route 30 onto Greensburg Pike Section 2 to Electric Avenue, where it met back up with Ardmore Boulevard in Chalfant.

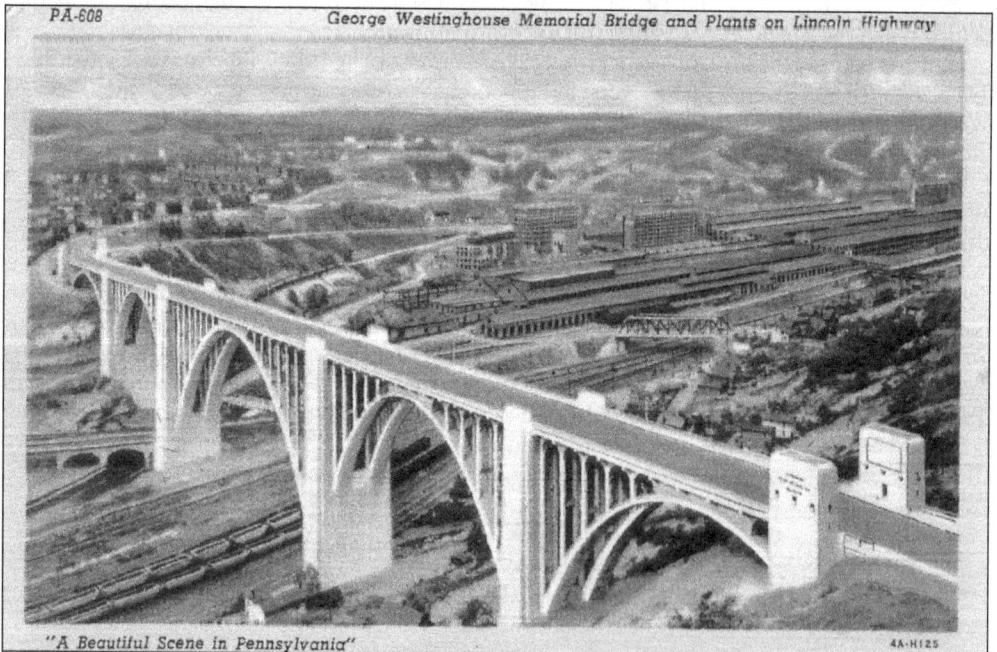

PA-608   George Westinghouse Memorial Bridge and Plants on Lincoln Highway

"A Beautiful Scene in Pennsylvania"   4A-H125

Penn Avenue, looking East,
Turtle Creek, Pa.

Although the Borough of Turtle Creek is just outside of the borders of this book's scope, the authors found this postcard image to be quite interesting. This is an eastward view along Penn Avenue. Trolley tracks (and a trolley) are visible in the middle of the road. (Allegheny Foothills Historical Society.)

About 12 miles east of downtown Pittsburgh, the George Westinghouse Memorial Bridge rises above what was then the Westinghouse Electrical Corporation's East Pittsburgh Works. The bridge has five spans, is over 1,500 feet long, cost about $1.75 million (approximately $30 million in 2014 money), and was built between 1929 and 1932. The bridge's grand opening was held on Saturday, September 10, 1932. (MRHHC.)

The railroad bridge that crosses Turtle Creek underneath the George Westinghouse Memorial Bridge was completely underwater in this photograph. The 1930s proved a difficult period (due to the Depression), and the Great St. Patrick's Day Flood of 1936 did not help. That year, torrential downpours on March 16 and 17 caused the rivers in the Pittsburgh region to rise as much as 21 feet over flood stage by March 18. (MRHHC.)

By 1880, the Pennsylvania Railroad terminal yards and shops in Pittsburgh were in need of expansion, although there was no room for expansion in the area. Railroad superintendent Robert Pitcairn decided to establish the new yard and transfer the engine house to the vicinity of Walls' Station. The new yard became known as the Pitcairn yard, located on the border of Wall between North Versailles and Pitcairn.

Above, workers prepare the molds for concrete to be poured along the banks of Turtle Creek in Wilmerding in an attempt to provide added flood control. A major flood struck Wilmerding in the 1950s, and after several years of debate and planning, a flood control plan was implemented by the Army Corps of Engineers to help alleviate the risk of flooding. Below is an image from the collections of the late Rudy Kukurin Sr., who spent the majority of his career working for various local construction firms (including the construction firm that worked on the aforementioned Wilmerding project). (Elaine Kukurin.)

This photograph of Westinghouse Park (later renamed Wilmerding Park) shows the Westinghouse "Castle" rising prominently in the background. The Castle was built in 1890 to serve as the general office of the Westinghouse Airbrake Company (WABCO). It also housed the personal office of George Westinghouse. An 1896 fire caused extensive damage to the Castle, but it was quickly rebuilt. In the latter part of the 20th century, under the management of Wilmerding Renewed, Inc., the Castle served as a museum for local and Westinghouse-related history for many years.

This photograph shows one of the earliest homes built in what is now Wilmerding. The borough of Wilmerding was named for Joanna Wilmerding Negley, wife of William B. Negley, who was a local landowner and nephew of Thomas Mellon. This image appeared in the 1940 publication *Golden Echoes: Official Publication Commemorating Wilmerding's 50th Anniversary Celebration*.

This image shows the broadcasting antenna for WPCB-TV, the flagship station of the Cornerstone TeleVision Network, which is based out of Wall. WPCB-TV began operations on April 15, 1979. Cornerstone TeleVision Network has over 100 full-power and low-power affiliates throughout the country. The photograph was taken in the vicinity of St. Joseph's Cemetery in North Versailles.

This is a postcard image of the old Wilmerding Public School building. On July 30, 1890, Mrs. A.M. Petty was elected principal of the school, with Elizabeth Kelly and Elizabeth Stamatz elected as assistants. When the first school term began in September of that year, classes were held in rented rooms in the Caesar Building on Herman Avenue. During this first term, the school had an enrollment of 109 students.

Westinghouse Memorial High School, Wilmerding, Pa.

Westinghouse Memorial High School served the community of Wilmerding prior to the creation of East Allegheny School District. After the merger with East Allegheny, high school classes were held solely at Westinghouse Memorial. In 1969, upon completion of the current high school, Westinghouse Memorial became an elementary school. When it closed at the end of the 2007–2008 school year, it was serving grades three through six.

Holy Trinity Byzantine Catholic Church began in 1928 when a committee met with Bishop Basil Takach for the purpose of receiving permission to create a parish in Wall. Takach granted permission for the construction of a hall to be used for services and social activities. The first Divine Liturgy was celebrated on April 28, 1929, by Fr. Arnold Suba of Rankin. The official opening of the parish did not take place until October 11, 1931, when Bishop Takach blessed the cornerstone. In 1964, the church purchased a neighboring house for use as a rectory.

Immigrants from a variety of ethnic backgrounds settled in the McKeesport area and the Turtle Creek valley. For those of Eastern and Southern European descent, this often meant having to travel long distances to attend services at a church that included fellow members of their ethnic group. In the image at right, new members of the Slovak Calvinist Presbyterian Church in Braddock make their first communion/confirmation; below, members of the Dency family, of Trafford, celebrate the wedding of Vilma Dency and Tom Kazmeraski. Long after moving into other areas (including North Versailles and Wilmerding), the Dency family continued to attend the Braddock church until its closure in the early 1960s. (Elaine Kukurin.)

Prior to the formation of Sts. Peter and Paul Ukrainian Greek Catholic Church in 1929, Byzantine Catholics in Wilmerding had to travel to McKeesport or Braddock in order to attend services. The congregation purchased this property on State Street from the St. John Vilna Lithuanian Society for $17,500. The dedication Mass (officiated by Rev. John Theodorovich, who was assisted by Rev. M. Machurak) was held in September 1929.

This image shows the Masonic Temple of Wilmerding around 1915. Freemasons are not the only fraternal organization that had a presence in the Wilmerding area. Other local fraternal groups included the Ancient Order of Hibernians, Wilmerding Temple No. 69 of the Pythian Sisters, and Lodge No. 1067 of the Independent Order of Odd Fellows (IOOF).

Masonic Temple, Wilmerding, Pa.

Five

SOUTH VERSAILLES TOWNSHIP

As South Versailles Township stands today, it is only a fraction of the size of the original South Versailles Township, with a current size of about one square mile and a population of about 350 people. Today, South Versailles is often locally referred to as Coulter (or Coulterville). However, what is now South Versailles is actually a collection of three small villages: Coulter, Osceola (also known as Emblem), and Alpsville. The community of Coulter drew its name from the original owners of the land, the Coulter family. Eli Coulter was given over 262 acres of land in 1787, and the family remained there for many generations. Col. Richard Coulter laid out the town, which was then called Coulters Narrows, in 1852. Other Coulter family members served in the military during the Civil War and served in state congress. In 1880, the population of Coulterville was around 882, a large number of whom earned their living in the mining industry.

Alpsville was primarily near St. Patrick's Church and surrounding hillsides. Near the church, prominent resident Nicholas J. Bigley built his family's home, the Bigley Mansion, which later served the community as a summer home for orphans.

Osceola—primarily located at the north/northwestern part of what is now South Versailles— received its name from a leader of the Seminole tribe. Osceola was the site of the first post office in the Coulterville area. In the vicinity of Alpsville and Osceola, Mr. N.J. Bigley operated Youghiogheny Collieries. Coal from his mines would then be transferred to Alpsville, where it was processed into industrial coke. In the mid-1800s, Youghiogheny Collieries had a daily output of 1,400 tons.

In addition to being the birthplace of Pittsburgh Steelers founder Art Rooney, South Versailles was also the birthplace of Major League Baseball's Joe "Moon" Harris. Harris played for several teams, including the Indians, Yankees, and Pirates. His career was briefly interrupted by his military service during World War I. Harris died in Plum Borough, in 1959, at age 68.

This railroad crossing along Eighth Street in Coulter is reminiscent of the role railroads once played in the community, serving as an integral part of the local coal mining industry. Some of the jobs created by the railroad and mining industries in South Versailles included pump house workers in Emblem, miners in the Osceola mine, and baggage handlers at the Coulter Passenger Station.

This 1890s photograph shows the Emblem Railroad Station. The first train ran through Emblem on January 14, 1857. There used to be water storage tanks in Emblem from the days when steam locomotives ruled the rails; engines would stop at these predetermined locations to take on coal and water. The advent of diesel locomotives in the 20th century eliminated the need for such stops. (John Barna.)

This image shows the Vandergrift Home of the Friendless in Alpsville. This institution began in 1894, when Capt. J.J. Vandergrift donated his property (formerly the Bigley Mansion) for use as a summer home for orphans. The dormitory had enough room for 120 boys. After the summer ended, the boys would return to the Pressley Street Orphanage in Pittsburgh. This facility closed in the early 1940s. (John Barna.)

Pictured here is the Coulter Inn during a particularly damaging fire. Although little information could be found about this business specifically, the Coulterville area had been serviced by several small hotels including the Shamrock Hotel, Rooney's Hotel, and Miscance Hotel. Apparently, the Miscance suffered a similar fate to the one pictured here, as it was consumed by fire in 1905. (Courtesy of the McKeesport Regional History and Heritage Center.)

ARTHUR J. ROONEY
(1901-1988)

Prominent Western Pennsylvania civic and sports leader and owner of the Pittsburgh Steelers, 1933-1988. With his guidance the Steelers won four 1970s Super Bowls. An accomplished athlete, Rooney was influential in the National Football League and was inducted into the National Football Hall of Fame, 1964. His family emigrated from Ireland in the 19th century; resided in Coulter where he was born until moving to Pittsburgh. He returned here often.

PENNSYLVANIA HISTORICAL AND MUSEUM COMMISSION   2005 ©

Coulter was once home to Art Rooney, founder of the Pittsburgh Steelers. Born in 1901, Rooney's parents moved the family to what is now the North Side of Pittsburgh while Art was young. After attending Duquesne University Preparatory School and graduating from college, "The Chief" went on to found the Pittsburgh Steelers football team. According to this historical marker, located at the intersection of School Street and Coulterville Road, Rooney visited Coulter often.

The Coulter Volunteer Fire Company was chartered on January 20, 1951, by 11 South Versailles citizens. The company's first fire truck was a Model T Ford (with a military pump) donated by Kennywood Park. The original fire hall was a building along Tourman Street that was purchased from Edward Reagan. The current building (pictured), located on Railroad Street, was completed in the 1990s.

In addition to one-room schools, many small churches dotted the landscape in both North and South Versailles Townships. The earliest incarnation of St. Patrick's Catholic Church stood in what is now locally known as Coulterville. The marker at right shows how the church looked around 1867, long before it was destroyed by fire in 1924. The church building was eventually reconstructed on the site (above), and the surrounding churchyard has been used as a family cemetery. In 1993, St. Patrick's merged with St. Denis of Versailles and St. Perpetua of McKeesport to form the new St. Patrick's Parish in McKeesport.

Original St. Patrick Church
CIRCA 1867
Destroyed by fire in 1924

In Memory of
Estelle M. Shepherd

1867

The St. Patrick's Catholic Church cemetery is slightly off the beaten path on Coulterville Road in South Versailles, and many members of the former church were laid to rest in this tranquil clearing in the woods. When the South Versailles church closed and merged with St. Denis Parish in McKeesport, the new parish retained the St. Patrick's name. Although the original St. Patrick's Church building (located on Tourman Street) no longer hosts services, the cemetery is still neatly maintained. The Elizabeth Township Historical Society maintains this cemetery as well as the nearby Coulter Cemetery.

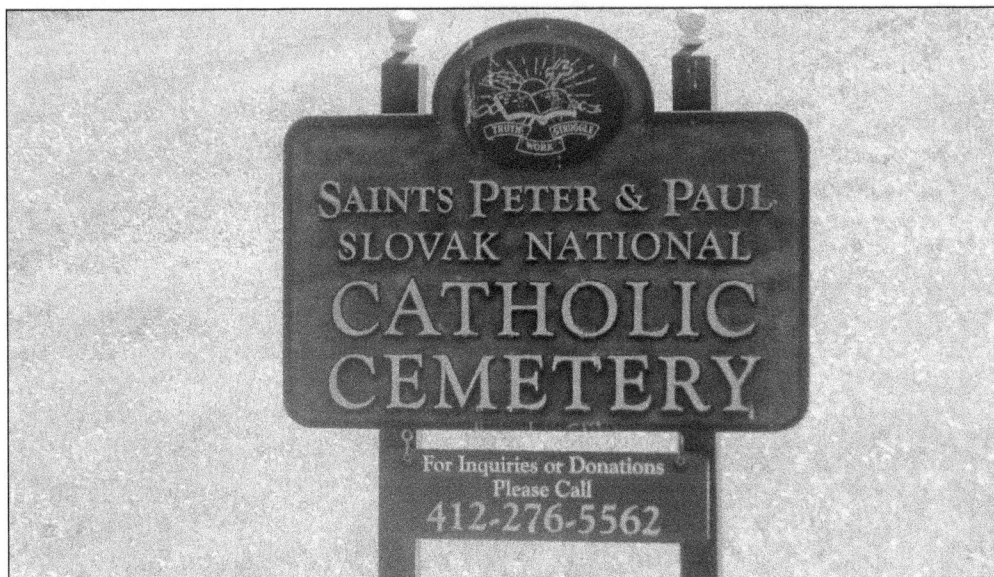

It is not unusual for congregations to have cemeteries far removed from their church buildings. In the case of Sts. Peter & Paul Slovak National Catholic Church of McKeesport, the congregation had a cemetery located along Coulterville Road, just off of Lincoln Way. The cemetery is still in existence and well maintained. The Slovak National Catholic Church was associated with the Polish National Catholic Church (PNCC). The PNCC has its roots in the late 19th century, when Polish immigrants to the United States became disillusioned with the hierarchy of the Roman Catholic Church. At that time, the Catholic Church in the United States had no Polish bishops and few Polish priests and would not allow the Polish language to be taught in parish schools. Franciszek Hodur (1866–1953) was consecrated a bishop by three Old Catholic bishops in Utrecht in 1907, thus forming the PNCC.

In 1892, the South Versailles Cemetery Association opened a secular burial ground along Coulterville Road, about midway between Lincoln Way in White Oak and the Art Rooney historical marker in central Coulterville. Several families that lived in the Coulter area are buried here. The cemetery is currently maintained by the Elizabeth Township Historical Society.

Six

VERSAILLES BOROUGH

The Borough of Versailles arose from the joining of two communities: Elrod and Bissel. In June 1892, residents of these two communities filed a petition with Allegheny County Courts. However, the proceedings were set aside by the courts until March 17, 1894. The incorporation of the new Versailles Borough was approved on June 16, 1894.

By this time, the area had been populated and the scene of industry for a number of years. A series of dams built in 1852 made the Youghiogheny River more easily navigable to points above Versailles. The dams only lasted about 10 years, at which time they were destroyed in a series of ice jams. Around 1870, a steamboat named *Boston*—owned and operated by Walter B. Harrison and Joseph Waltower—provided transportation between the Market Street Wharf in McKeesport and Greenock (Elizabeth Township). At least two other boats were purchased by Joseph Waltower in subsequent years: Scout and Nellie England.

In 1875, a railroad from Connellsville to McKeesport was laid through the area. By 1880, the railroad had provided sufficient competition to the steamboat company that the steamboats ceased operating. That same year, the Lake Erie Railroad was completed on the Boston side of the Youghiogheny River. By 1882, a railroad station was in place just below the Boston Bridge.

Many factors contributed to the growth of Versailles Borough. Its placement along the river—very close to the industrial strips in McKeesport—played a vital role, along with the availability of housing, an education system, and transportation. During the earliest days of Versailles, students attended one of two schools—The Hawthorne School at Osceola or Long Run School (located in present-day White Oak).

The Versailles Traction Company incorporated in 1892. Most lines in the area were taken over in 1916 by West Penn Railways. The borough increased in size from around 100 houses, in the 1890s, to over 400 in 1930. The population grew exponentially during the same period—from a few hundred to 2,400.

Although the Monongahela Valley is best known for its steel industry, the gas industry also played a major role in its history. Pictured above are some of the gas wells located in Versailles Borough. Over 650 gas wells were drilled in and around the McKeesport area, mostly during the McKeesport "gas boom" that lasted from 1919 to 1925. The gas boom caused such hype that the number of companies drilling wells went from 116 in 1919 to 297 by mid-January 1920. Below is another photograph of a privately owned gas well situated next to a residence. (MRHHC.)

Pictured at right is a fenced lot containing a gas well, piping, and other random gas-related equipment. Although few people could have imagined the hoopla that would arise in the years after the Spiegel Gas Well was struck in July 1915 in North Versailles, the finances of the drilling did not quite add up. An estimated $13 million was spent drilling the McKeesport Gas Field, which contained just a little over $3 million of gas. In the below image, several gas wells are visible in the distance. (MRHHC.)

This photograph offers another view of some of the many gas wells that spread across the region in the early 20th century. This photograph is believed to have been taken in the vicinity of Walnut Street in Versailles Borough. (MRHHC.)

So excited was the atmosphere during the gas boom, that landowners, stockholders, and drillers would hold so-called "gas baby parties" while they waited for wells to come online. During some of the "gas baby" parties in and around Versailles, things got so frenzied that several explosions occurred. Seven homes were destroyed, and rumors swirled about several hundred people injured. Mayor George Lysle, of neighboring McKeesport, pushed for a ban on the practice of holding such parties. (MRHHC.)

Here are two more images of the gas wells that arose in and around Versailles. These photographs offer an interesting accompaniment to local news accounts of the time, in which journalists described the practice of holding "gas baby parties" prior to christening a new well. As early as 1920, geological surveyors were warning drillers that investments currently being made (in 1920) would most likely result in total losses—or at the very least, near-total losses. The warnings were very rarely heeded, however, and the drilling persisted. (MRHHC.)

This photograph, taken from across the Youghiogheny River, offers an incredible, sweeping view of the gas wells in Versailles. The Youghiogheny once served as a navigable river for industry. In 1850, a series of locks and dams were constructed, allowing boats to utilize more of the river. In the early 1860s, an ice gorge destroyed the dams. Although the dams were never rebuilt, the Army Corps of Engineers did consider damming the river again in 1910. Dredging of a navigable boating lane was again discussed in 1971. (MRHHC.)

This photograph of the 4400 block of Walnut Street shows more of the gas wells that sprang up in Versailles. The brick house at left still exists and is currently an insurance agent's office. One problem that arose in Versailles was the burning gob pile that existed under what became the Ames parking lot. The gob pile was the result of industrial waste from the Hubbard Mine (at the western end of Third Street) being destroyed by fire. (MRHHC.)

This photograph shows the Long Run Bridge, near Walnut Street, which was built in 1906 by Allegheny County. The following people's names were placed on the placard commemorating the bridge's opening: Chas. B. Price, I.K. Campbell, commissioners; J.A.Clark, F.P. Booth, controllers; Chas. Davis, engineer; O.C. Litterio, builder. (John Barna.)

This is a bridge near the mouth of Long Run Creek. The Baltimore & Ohio Railroad once crossed the stream near here. Long Run is known to have a few ponds deep enough to sustain fish and is on the state's list of approved trout-stocked streams. (John Barna.)

Railroad workers pose with an engine on a Baltimore & Ohio turntable in Versailles. The Baltimore & Ohio Railroad was the first Class I railroad in the country. During its height, the railroad extended as far east as Staten Island, New York, and as far west as Illinois. (John Barna.)

In this undated photograph, officials gather to break ground for a railroad bridge near Versailles (possibly the bridge crossing over Douglas Street). Generally, transportation improvements were not made in Versailles until well into the 1940s and 1950s. Prior to mid-century, unimproved roads were merely given a yearly coat of oil. By the 1960s, most streets and alleyways were paved. (MRHHC.)

The Boston Bridge—the connector between Versailles Borough and Elizabeth Township—was still under construction in this photograph. The 1,181-foot-long, 30-foot-wide bridge was completed in 1931. The old Boston Bridge is visible on the right. Originally, travelers paid a toll on the old bridge—5¢ for pedestrians and 25¢ for teamster wagons. (MRHHC.)

Olympia Park, which opened around 1900, is a classic example of a trolley park—a park built along (or at the end of) a trolley line in order to increase the number of riders along a particular route. This postcard offers a view of the Colonial Inn. (MRHHC.)

The Colonial Inn in Olympia Park served many purposes during its tenure, including that of hotel, restaurant, and as a residence for the park manager. National Tube Works often used the inn as a club for company officials and their guests. (MRHHC.)

This roller coaster in Olympia Park served patrons until 1921, at which point it was replaced with a new coaster called the Leap Frog. Tracks for the park's miniature railway are visible in the lower right corner. (MRHHC.)

Front View of Olympia Park,
McKeesport, Pa.

This grassy field originally served as the parking lot for Olympia Park visitors. By the mid-1920s, the park had installed an improved parking where the ball field originally stood. Prior to the park's construction, a farm belonging to the Bissell family once occupied this area. (MRHHC.)

In 1901, the Pittsburgh, McKeesport & Connellsville Railway Company purchased the land that became Olympia Park. This is the back of Colonial Inn in Olympia Park. The women's restroom is at right. (MRHHC.)

Generations of students have memories of going to places like Kennywood and Idlewild for school picnics. Both present-day students and early-20th-century groups went on such outings at places like Olympia Park. This photograph (split into two pieces for this book's layout) captures the members of the congregation of St. Stephen's Episcopal Church, who had their picture taken

...phen's Episcopal Church Outing.

during a July 23, 1929, outing at Olympia Park. The first Episcopal service in McKeesport was held in 1869. In 1871, a mission church was created for 33 confirmed members of the Episcopal church. St. Stephen's was incorporated as an independent parish on Nov. 3, 1885. (MRHHC.)

An unidentified family poses on a bridge that once stood in Olympia Park. In addition to some amusement rides, Olympia Park also had a picnic area, a lake for boating, the Rollerdome, and Danceland. The park closed in 1942, and the lake was later drained. (MRHHC.)

This photograph of the Versailles Council No. 691 group of the Independent Order of Odd Fellows (IOOF) State Entertainment Committee was taken during the group's 16th annual convention, which was held in McKeesport on September 2, 3, and 4, 1919. Markings on the photograph indicate that one of the gentlemen is William B. Stevick. (MRHHC.)

Pictured here are two classes from the old Versailles Borough School. The Versailles Borough School was built in 1900 between Larch and Juniper Streets. The building originally housed four rooms spread over two stories. The school was later expanded, and it eventually housed grades one through eight. In 1980, the school was torn down to make room for a 24-room senior apartment complex, which was dedicated on May 1, 1983. The borough was actually served by several schools throughout its early history. The first school to have been built in the borough was on Chestnut, near where the military Honor Roll presently sits. The second school that was founded was located in a building that later became Price's and Bowden's Grocery Stores. (The grocery store was later bought by the fire department and demolished.) (MRHHC.)

In this 1894 photograph, a man in a horse-drawn buggy travels across a bridge over Long Run Creek while another man stands in the creek bed. It is not known precisely where this bridge was located along the creek. (John Barna.)

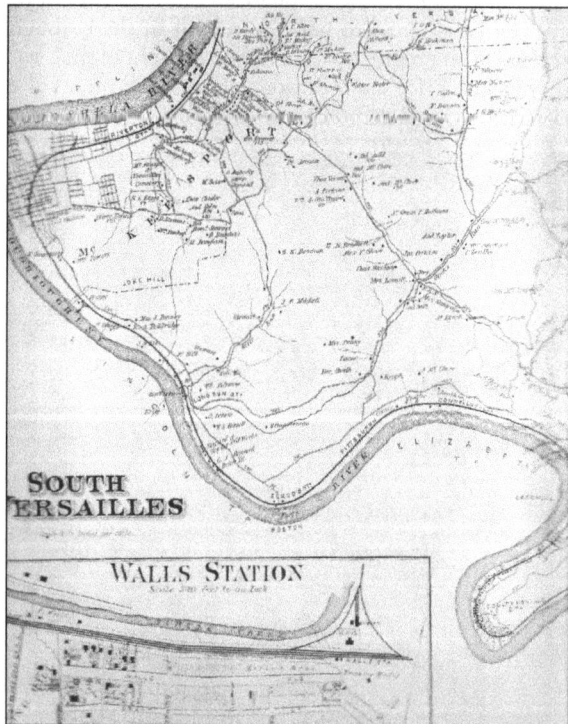

SOUTH
VERSAILLES

WALLS STATION

As depicted in the 1988 reprint of the 1876 *Atlas of the County of Allegheny, Penna.*, South Versailles (of which Versailles Borough was a part) was obviously much more rural in the late 19th century. "Wall's Station" (Wall Borough—discussed earlier in this book) is shown in the lower inset. (Thomas and Katherine Detre Library and Archives—Senator John Heinz History Center and the Allegheny Foothills Historical Society.)

Seven

WHITE OAK BOROUGH

The area that became White Oak was the last remnant of the old Versailles Township. Through World War II, the area maintained its semirural feel. After the war, the presence of improved transportation routes and many more jobs available than during the Depression made Versailles Township a very attractive place to live.

The formation of White Oak was not without its troubles. Residents of certain sections of Versailles Township (including Bryn Mawr, Amherst Terrace, and the Summit-Fawcett-Franklin plans) wished to be annexed by the city of McKeesport. Others in the township believed the incorporation of a new borough was the best course of action, while yet others wished the township would stay as is.

The final petition requesting the formation of White Oak Borough was submitted on March 21, 1948. On June 24, 1948, Judge Russell H. Adams signed the decree of incorporation during the Quarter Sessions Court. The first borough building was located at 860 Maple Street inside the old Bowery School. In 1971, the local government unveiled plans for a new borough building, which was completed and dedicated in 1973.

The area that became White Oak is perhaps best known for being home to the former Rainbow Gardens amusement park. Rainbow Gardens, known as a favorite recreational spot for local families for decades, was perhaps equally famous for its demise. In late 1968, Rainbow Gardens fell victim to eminent domain—the property was to be used for the construction of a cloverleaf interchange for an expanded State Route 48 Expressway. Due to funding issues, the road project never came to fruition, and the property lay dormant until Oak Park Mall was constructed there in the early 1990s.

These miniatures of paintings originally done by George L. Sloane depict scenes from around what is now White Oak. Clockwise from the top left are the Hartman Estate in Bryn Mawr, Rainbow Gardens, Stewarts Market, Lincoln School, the first-grade building for Bryn Mawr School, Bryn Mawr School, Edlow's Grocery Store, and Mehaffey's Gas Station. (Jim and Linda Wetzler.)

This mid-1870s photograph shows the house of Andrew and Mary Kelly McClure. Andrew was a descendant of Francis McClure, a Revolutionary War soldier and judge. Kelly Street, in White Oak, was named in honor of Mary Kelly McClure. (MRHHC.)

This photograph of the Fawcett family's Franklin Street home was taken on August 2, 1879. Pictured here are, from left to right (as identified on the back of the photograph), "one of Grandfather Fawcett's brothers, William G. Fawcett; grandmother; grandfather; Mina. Danny Bennett and Cora Fawcett are peeking out of the window." (MRHHC.)

William G. Fawcett stands near the fence while other family members pose in the barn's upper entrances. The barn was in the vicinity of the 1100 block of Fawcett Avenue. The original Fawcett farm consisted of 116 acres purchased from of William Whigham, who had named his property the Pleasant Valley Farm. (MRHHC.)

The house shown in the background belonged to the Bailey family. The Baileys, who owned this property located at what later became the intersection of State Route 48 and Lincoln Way, rented out the log house, which eventually burned down. This photograph was taken around 1922. (John Barna.)

The Weddell farmhouse (pictured) was part of the land eventually purchased by Allegheny County to form White Oak Regional Park. The house was built sometime in the late 19th century and has four rooms on both the first and second floors, each with its own fireplace. Five generations of the Weddell family lived in this house. (John Barna.)

This c. 1910 photograph looks down O'Neil Boulevard from Franklin Street. The railroad and trolleys played a major role in local industries. The Pittsburgh & Connellsville Railroad (later absorbed into the Baltimore & Ohio Railroad) built a line that runs through a part of what is now White Oak; by 1861, the line was extended to Pittsburgh. (MRHHC.)

This 1910 image shows an almost unrecognizable photograph, taken from somewhere around the future location of Mann's Drug Store, of the intersection of Lincoln Way and O'Neil Boulevard. The house at right now contains a doctor's office. At the time, Lincoln Way had trolleys traveling on it. (MRHHC.)

The gas boom reached into the heart of what became White Oak. Pictured here are some of the wells that sprang up in the vicinity of Sampson's Mills Presbyterian Church. The wells reached depths of 2,400 to 4,000 feet. Note the trolley track faintly visible in the foreground—this line took passengers to Irwin. This photograph was taken around 1918. (MRHHC.)

This photograph of the McKeesport Cyclers was taken around 1910 on the Long Run Bridge at Sampson's Mill, near where Rainbow Gardens was located. A herd of cattle are watering themselves in the creek. Note the horse and buggy on the bridge—automobiles were still in their early years at this point in time. (MRHHC.)

In this image, taken shortly after the start of the 20th century, an unidentified man stands beside his car near the old Congress Street Bridge in White Oak. The W.E. Hartman house (built in the late 19th century) is visible across the bridge in the Bryn Mawr section of town. (MRHHC.)

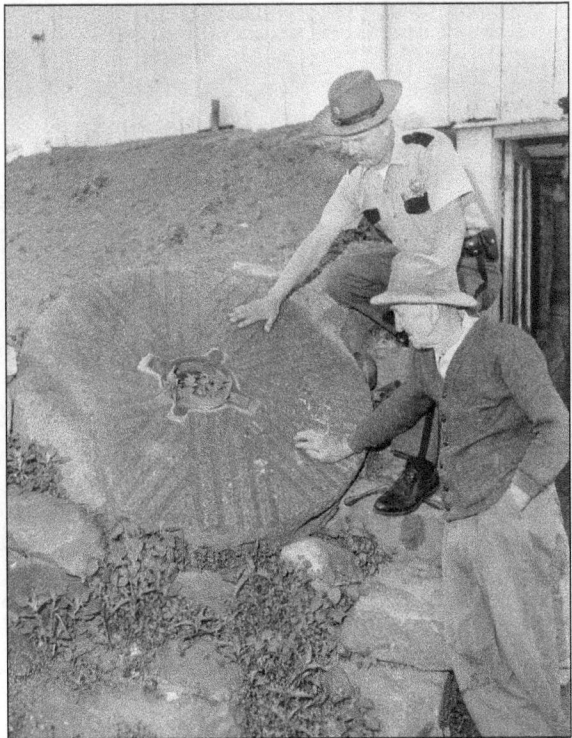

Luke Ripple and a Mr. Miller inspect one of the millstones on the Ripple farm. Millstones from the old Sampson's Mill are currently located in front of Sampson's Mill Presbyterian Church and by the bank in Rainbow Shopping Center. (MRHHC.)

Presbyterians began worshiping in what is now White Oak in 1893, and Sampson's Mill Presbyterian Church constructed its first building in 1902. From the 1930s to the 1950s, the congregation's population doubled from 225 to 450, leading to talks of expansion. The Christian education building (built in 1957) and the sanctuary (built in 1972) are visible in this image.

DIRECTORY OF

TRINITY
EV. LUTHERAN CHURCH

The Rev. Martin J. Roth, Pastor

Salem Street & Stewart Avenue
McKeesport, Pennsylvania 15132
Phone: 672-6094

1523 Kansas Avenue, White Oak
McKeesport, Pennsylvania 15131
Phone: 673-7945

Although Faith Lutheran Church of White Oak was not founded until 1972, it has a long history because of the three churches that merged to form it—Tabor Lutheran Church (founded January 23, 1887) and Trinity Lutheran Church (both of McKeesport), plus Calvary Lutheran of White Oak. (Faith Lutheran Church.)

Calvary Lutheran was the newest of the three congregations that merged to form Faith Lutheran Church. When it was originally organized on August 16, 1953, the Calvary congregation included 30 families who met in a house on Hemlock Drive in White Oak. The first pastor, William Steiner, was called to serve in November 1953. Reverend Steiner is pictured above leading a church service. (Faith Lutheran Church.)

The new Calvary Lutheran building was dedicated on Reformation Sunday, October 28, 1962. The ceremony held on that day was probably much like the one pictured here (Organization Day on November 15, 1963). In October 1972, the leaders of Calvary, Tabor, and Trinity Lutheran decided that a merger was in the best interest of all parties, and a charter for Faith Lutheran Church of McKeesport was officially put forth. (Faith Lutheran Church.)

Pictured here is the steering committee for the new Faith Lutheran Church. One of the decisions made by early church leaders dealt with the search for a pastor. Rev. Arthur Ackerman was called in October 1973 to serve the new congregation. (Faith Lutheran Church.)

In April 1981, eight years after the merger that formed Faith Lutheran Church, the congregation approved a plan to construct an addition to their small church building. The house that had served as the parish house (located at 1656 Lincoln Way) was demolished, and construction began on an addition to the church building. The addition—which contains classrooms, a social hall, and a lounge—was dedicated in May 1982. (MRHHC.)

Prior to the formation of St. Angela Merici Catholic Church and school in White Oak, Lee's Barn (pictured) served as a venue for religious education and catechism. This structure replaced the church's need to hold classes in the White Oak American Legion building. (St. Angela Merici Catholic Church.)

PROPOSED ARCHITECTURAL RENDERINGS

ST. ANGELA'S
NEW SCHOOL
And
CHURCH

WORK...

This is the original architect's rendering of St. Angela Merici Church and school buildings. St. Angela's began holding Mass on June 15, 1958, at the Rainbow Gardens Roller Rink. The ground-breaking ceremony for the new school and "temporary" church building occurred on July 24, 1960, and the first Mass was held in the new building on August 20, 1961. (St. Angela Merici Catholic Church.)

Fr. Cyril Drapp was called in 1969 to serve St. Angela's Parish. During his six-year tenure, he oversaw fundraising for the building of a parish activities center. Unfortunately, Father Drapp suddenly passed away on September 27, 1975. When ground was broken for the new activities center on November 1, 1975, the congregation decided that the center would be named in honor of Father Drapp. (St. Angela Merici Catholic Church.)

In 2001, the new bell tower for St. Angela's Parish was lowered into place as the new sanctuary neared completion. The bell itself was manufactured by McShane Bell Company of Baltimore, Maryland. The bell tower was a gift to the church from Mascaro Construction Company. The new church additions were dedicated on January 26, 2002. (St. Angela Merici Catholic Church.)

Members of Bryn Mawr Church of Christ are pictured making apple butter in the church's yard. Those identified in the photograph include Mary Schoeller and Bill Yahn. The land used for the church's current building was purchased in 1918, with the church purchasing additional land in 1926. The church building was completed in 1928. (MRHHC.)

Jack's Run School was built in the vicinity of Jack's Run (hence its name), near where McClintock Road now intersects with State Route 48. The original Jack's Run School was built in the early 19th century but later dismantled. The building pictured here was constructed around 1870 and served the community until its closure in 1930. (MRHHC.)

This photograph (detailed below) of the Bryn Mawr Christian Church's Bible School was taken on June 5, 1927. The congregation, which later changed its name to Bryn Mawr Church of Christ, had its earliest incarnation in 1894, when a group of residents organized the Union Sabbath School. Some of those identified in this photograph include Araminta Schneider Schultz, James

TIAN CHURCH - JUNE 5, 1927

Schneider, and Mary Margaret Schneider-Decker (holding baby Isabel Decker Garrett). Rev. W.C. McDonald is third from the left on the second row of people standing in front of the doorway. The building pictured here was an old schoolhouse donated to the congregation in 1902 by National Tube Works. (MRHHC.)

URCH ~ JUNE, 5, 1927

Gemilas Chesed Synagogue was founded in 1886 in what was then the Third Ward of McKeesport. The Gemilas Chesed congregation moved to their current worship site (above) in 1963. When moving from their McKeesport building, the pews, bimah and aron kodesh (podium and Torah ark) were also brought along to the new building. Below several members of the congregation are pictured. During the heyday of the McKeeport's industrial boom, the area's Jewish population is said to have been one of the largest Jewish communities in the United States, behind only New York. Gemilas Chesed is also home to the Gemilas Chesed Sisterhood. Led by the group's first president Mrs. Albert (Edith) Gross, the organization was born from the Ladies Auxiliary and was organized in 1961. (MRHHC.)

Pictured here are students from the Bryn Mawr School. Bryn Mawr—built in the 1890s—replaced the one-room Shaw School built in the early 1800s. Originally a four-room building, Bryn Mawr later added a cafeteria and indoor plumbing in 1948. As enrollment increased, the first grade was moved to the building which later became the White Oak Rescue Building. Bryn Mawr School was destroyed by a fire in 1956. (MRHHC.)

When Lincoln School first opened along Ohio Avenue in 1916, it only had four classrooms and an office. As more room was needed, four more rooms and a cafeteria were added. Even a portable classroom was constructed in the 1930s for use by a single class. It was dismantled in the 1950s when White Oak School was built. When Lincoln School was closed, it was then converted into an apartment complex. (MRHHC.)

Pictured above is an aerial view of the old Fawcett Avenue School. Designed by Henry Lohman of McKeesport, excavating for Fawcett School began in 1905. The school opened in 1907. Seen below, a group of Fawcett Avenue School students pose outside of their school to have their photograph taken. While Fawcett Avenue School was torn down sometime in the 1980s, other schools still exist along the Fawcett-Summit corridor. St. Angela Merici School (now Mon Yough Catholic School) on Fawcett began in the early 1960s, initially with just first and second grades. It now educates students in grades Kindergarten through eight. The Gemilas Chesed Synagogue on Summit Avenue hosts a Mesivta (secondary school) for boys in grades nine through twelve. (MRHHC.)

Proposed in 1953, Francis McClure Junior High School was built in 1959. The building's original capacity was slated at around 850 students. Although the school was originally meant to be a junior high school servicing grades six through nine, the school was later changed to a "Middle School" serving grades five through eight. (MRHHC.)

Wood shop teacher Ron Burns is seen sharing a laugh with a student teacher in this photograph. Prior to his retirement in 1997, he supervised over 100 industrial arts student teachers during his 37-year teaching career. He also received the Pennsylvania Outstanding Industrial Arts Teacher of the Year Award in 1984. (MRHHC.)

Students of Francis McClure School were attentively learning about the various tools they would have to utilize during their time in the school's wood shop. (The elder of the two authors has many fond memories of working in this wood shop). Pictured below, a student is seen hard at work using a hand plane. Unfortunately, the school no longer has an industrial arts program. However, the rooms that were once the wood and metal shops are still in use as classrooms. (MRHHC.)

Pictured here are scenes from Francis McClure's metal shop. Above, instructor Dan Piesik shows two students how to operate a piece of machinery. Note the "M&M" poster on the wall in the upper left corner. This is not an advertisement for the famous candy brand. It reads "Metalworking & Manners—Made in USA." Below, two students concentrate on properly forming their metalwork. (MRHHC.)

White Oak School was built in 1950 with 10 classrooms for use by grades one through six and a cafeteria/auditorium room. After the 1955 addition was completed, an earth fault was discovered as the cause of some cracks which appeared in the cafeteria walls. However, authorities determined students were not at risk. (MRHHC.)

Mike Kordalski is pictured during the annual White Oak Elementary School Halloween parade in front of the school. White Oak School has gone through several renovations over the years. Originally built in 1950, the school started out with 10 rooms plus an auditorium/cafeteria. An additional 12 rooms were added in 1955. Two other additions were completed around 1990 and 2000.

Pictured here are the First and Second Grade classes of St. Angela Merici School in 1961. St. Angela's school began on September 10, 1961, and was staffed by the Sisters of the Congregation of St. Joseph (whose motherhouse is located in Baden, Pennsylvania). Sister M. Carmella served as both the first grade teacher and principal. She was later joined by second grade teacher Sister M. Agatha. In 2012, St. Angela's school merged with St. Joseph Regional Catholic School (founded in Port Vue in 1984) to form Mon-Yough Catholic School. The current school operates out of the St. Angela building and services eight parishes. (St. Angela Merici Catholic Church.)

Pictured above, Rudy Kukurin poses inside of his earthmover during a winter job. Although neither of these photographs was geographically identified, the photograph below reminds the authors of their imagining of what the Baker Plan of White Oak may have looked like while still being developed. The Baker farm, which was made up of parcels bought from the John W. Guice and Andrew McClure properties, was primarily a horse farm. Sarah Mildred Clark married Wesley Baker, but later returned to Versailles Township after Wesley disappeared. It was at this point that Sarah began her property acquisitions. Rudy Kukurin Sr. worked for the contractor who developed part of the Baker Plan. (Elaine Kukurin.)

The building boom of the late 1940s and 1950s continued as the baby boomers came of age in the 1960s and 1970s. Many of the local farms that had provided fresh produce for generations had been sold off and purchased by housing developers. Photographed around 1977, Frank and Karen Kordalski stand in the not-yet-complete foundation of their house on what used to be a part of the Baker Family farm in White Oak. As is evident from the spray-painted number, the "job number" of this house was 424.

The gas company seen here belongs to Peoples Natural Gas Co. (located at the intersection of Ripple Road and Route 48). The alpine structure in the photograph started in the 1920s as the Flower Garden which later became LaRosa Gardens. Long Run Tavern is the structure on the bottom left. (MRHHC.)

Dougherty's Restaurant along Route 48 is seen in this mid-20th-century photograph. The men on the right side of the photograph are apparently inspecting the road around the retaining wall along Long Run. The maintenance shed is blocking the view of Ripple Road as it comes down from Center Street. (MRHHC.)

Flooding on June 18, 1956 left the intersection of Lincoln Way and Route 48 under water. This inundation was the second such event in four days, and at its height it covered the intersection in three feet of water. Two feet of mud was left in Rainbow Garden's swimming pool. Overall, about $150,000 worth of damage was done to the community. (MRHHC.)

The corner of State Street and Lincoln Way was a major pocket of commerce in 1953. This is William Mehaffey's Garage, which was next to Stalling's Dairy and Edlow's Market. (MRHHC.)

Pictured here is the Landstorm residence along Foster Road. It was later purchased by the Moore family. Foster Road is named for (you guessed it) the Foster family. Samuel D. Foster purchased a farm in 1834. The Fosters also mined coal off of what is now Capitol Street. (MRHHC.)

What was, at the time, Club Belvedere, was briefly considered for purchase by Calvary Lutheran as a possible site for their new church. By September 1955, the congregation instead purchased the property at 1656 Lincoln Way. The house on this property was dedicated as a House Chapel on April 29, 1956. In May 1960, the congregation purchased the adjacent property on Lincoln Way which eventually became the site of the new church building. Ground breaking took place on February 25, 1962. (Faith Lutheran Church.)

Club Belvedere—later known as the White Elephant and the Dynasty—was a popular place for teenagers to go on weekends for dances and other such functions. Various popular local disc jockeys (such as Porky Chedwick, Barry Kaye, and Jay Michael) performed their magic with the turntables at this venue. (Faith Lutheran Church.)

Pictured here are two officers of White Oak's Police Department standing next to their squad car. The borough's police department was a small one when it first began. During the 1950s, one would have to call McKeesport's dispatcher at 8-6186 and request "car 120." Now hooked up to the regional 911 dispatch system, White Oak's Police force has 10 full-time officers, two part-time officers, and eight police cars. (MRHHC.)

As one local resident stated in White Oak's 50th anniversary book, kids growing up in White Oak during the 1950s "had their own personal playground at Rainbow Gardens." Eventually, Rainbow Gardens included a swimming pool, a roller skating rink, miniature golf, and various amusement park rides. In 1927, McKeesport businessman John "Pete" Hoerr and his son John gained control of the corporation which planned on developing the Rainbow Gardens and proceeded with their plans for the park. Some of the attractions which the park was known for include the 170 foot by 270 foot swimming pool, dance pavilion, picnic grounds, and a row of cottages on the hill behind the pool. Local farmer George Kitz was asked to dig out the pool area—which he did with a team of horses and a hand-operated scoop. (MRHHC.)

Pictured here is the roller coaster, which became the highlight of Rainbow Gardens. Built in 1954, the coaster had a price tag of $60,000. By this point in time, the Versailles Amusement Company was in control of the park. On July 4, 1928, a tremendous storm flooded the park, leaving the pool in a muddy state of disarray. The Hoerr family's corporation could not survive the financial blow and filed for bankruptcy on September 26, 1928. Sometime after the stock market crash of 1929, historical accounts indicate the Hoerrs lost the property in a sheriff's sale. The Versailles Amusement Company also oversaw the installation of the drive-in theater in 1947. (MRHHC.)

Pictured here are two more rides that were especially popular amongst children and families—the train and the "little" Roto-Whip. The park's most successful period was during the 1950s and 1960s. During this time, one could buy a ride-all-day pass for $2. Many schools and companies held their annual picnics here; the National Tube Company's picnic would draw about 20,000 patrons to the park. Unfortunately, the park met its end in the face of progress. The state's Department of Transportation had plans of expanding Route 48 into an expressway of sorts, and would utilize the land surrounding Rainbow Gardens for a cloverleaf interchange. Imminent domain prevailed and the park was ordered to be vacated. On November 1, 1968, all of the rides and many other items within the park were auctioned off. (MRHHC.)

The Tilt-a-Whirl sold for about $14,000 when the contents of the park were auctioned off. Despite all of the money invested in procuring properties for the Route 48 expressway, money for road construction began to dry up and the plans for the expressway were halted. It took over 20 years before the Rainbow Gardens property returned to the tax rolls. In the park's place, Oak Park Mall was constructed. (MRHHC.)

A woman's near-perfect dive is caught in this photograph as she enters the water of Rainbow Gardens' Pool. Taken around 1950, this photograph also captures the park's roller coaster in the background. During the park's later years, it hosted a Wild Mouse–style roller coaster. (MRHHC.)

Looking east, this December 1955 photograph shows a much different view of Lincoln Way than we are used to today. The Rainbow Gardens Drive-In Theatre once only cost $1 per vehicle. Both the theatre and the Dairy Queen pictured here were eventually demolished as part of the defunct Route 48 Expressway plan. (MRHHC.)

It is only fitting that we finish out this book with a photograph of two of those to whom we have dedicated this book. Bitsy (left) and Pikachu (right) stand guard over the long-since completed house featured earlier in this chapter. If they were still with us (and could read), certainly they would hope you enjoyed reading this book as much as we enjoyed writing it!

BIBLIOGRAPHY

Atlas of the County of Allegheny: 1988 Reprint Edition. (Pittsburgh: The Historical Society of Western Pennsylvania)

The East McKeesport Centennial Book (East McKeesport, 1995)

Golden Echoes: Official Publication Commemorating Wilmerding's 50th Anniversary Celebration. (Wilmerding: 1940).

Golden Memories of Coulter, Alpsville and Osceola (South Versailles, Penn.: Coulter Book Committee, 1997)

History of Allegheny County, Pennsylvania (Chicago: A. Warner & Co., 1889)

McKeesport Heritage Center Volunteers. Images of America: *McKeesport.* (Charleston, SC: Arcadia Publishing, 2007).

Memories [1894–1994]: Versailles Borough Centennial (Versailles Borough, Penn.: Versailles Borough Historical Committee, 1994)

Wardle-Eggers, Michelle Tryon and John W. Barna. Postcard History Series: *McKeesport.* (Charleston, SC: Arcadia Publishing, 2011).

White Oak—50 Years: An Historical Perspective (Trust Frankling Press Company: 1998)

Wilmerding Renewed. Images of America: *Wilmerding and the Westinghouse Air Brake Company.* (Charleston, SC: Arcadia Publishing, 2002).

ABOUT THE MCKEESPORT REGIONAL HISTORY AND HERITAGE CENTER

The McKeesport Regional History and Heritage Center operates a museum and research facility dedicated to preserving and presenting the history of McKeesport and its surrounding communities (including those in the former Versailles Township). The center is located in Renzie Park at 1832 Arboretum Drive, McKeesport, Pennsylvania, 15132. Please consider donating any documents, photographs, maps, books, or other memorabilia from areas covered in this book for future generations to enjoy. Current hours of operation can be found on their website (www.mckeesportheritage.org) or by calling (412) 678-1832.

Visit us at
arcadiapublishing.com

· ·